Experiencing Speech: A Skills-Based, Panlingual Approach to Actor Training

Experiencing Speech: A Skills-Based, Panlingual Approach to Actor Training is a beginner's guide to Knight-Thompson Speechwork®, a method that focuses on universal and inclusive speech training for actors from all language, racial, cultural, and gender backgrounds and identities.

This book provides a progression of playful, practical exercises designed to build a truly universal set of speech skills that any actor can use, such as the ability to identify, discern, and execute every sound found in every language on the planet. By observing different types of flow through the vocal tract, vocal tract anatomy, articulator actions, and how these components can be combined, readers will understand and recreate the process by which language is learned. They will then be introduced to the International Phonetic Alphabet (IPA) and will practice using the IPA for narrow transcription of speech sounds. The book also offers both an intellectual and physical understanding of oral posture and how it contributes to vocal characterization and accent work. This approach to speech training is descriptive, giving students a wide and diverse set of speech sounds and skills to utilize for any character in any project, and it establishes a foundation for future accent study and acquisition.

Experiencing Speech: A Skills-Based, Panlingual Approach to Actor Training is an excellent resource for teachers and students of speech and actor training, as well as aspiring actors looking to diversify their speech skills.

Andrea Caban is Co-Director of Knight-Thompson Speechwork®, is Associate Professor and Head of Voice and Speech at CSU Long Beach, and holds a research appointment at UC Irvine in the Department of

Neurology. She is the accent expert on HowCast.com demonstrating over 35 accents, a regular speaker coach for TED, and a recipient of the Dudley Knight Award for Outstanding Vocal Scholarship. For more information, visit www.andreacaban.com.

Julie Foh is Assistant Professor of Voice and Speech at the University of Connecticut, a member of the Voice and Speech Trainers Association, and Associate Teacher of Fitzmaurice Voicework. She is a certified teacher of Knight-Thompson Speechwork® and a professional voice and dialect coach.

Jeffrey Parker is Associate Professor of Theatre at Metropolitan State University of Denver and a certified teacher of Knight-Thompson Speechwork®. He is a member of the Voice and Speech Trainers Association and the current Director of Voice and Text at the Colorado Shakespeare Festival.

Experiencing Speech: A Skills-Based, Panlingual Approach to Actor Training

A Beginner's Guide to Knight-Thompson Speechwork®

Andrea Caban, Julie Foh,
and Jeffrey Parker

Routledge
Taylor & Francis Group

NEW YORK AND LONDON

First published 2021
by Routledge
52 Vanderbilt Avenue, New York, NY 10017

and by Routledge
2 Park Square, Milton Park, Abingdon, Oxon, OX14 4RN

Routledge is an imprint of the Taylor & Francis Group, an informa business

© 2021 Taylor & Francis

Library of Congress Cataloging-in-Publication Data
Names: Caban, Andrea, author. | Foh, Julie, author. | Parker, Jeffrey
      (Jeffrey B.), author.
Title: Experiencing speech : a skills-based, panlingual approach to actor
      training / Andrea Caban, Julie Foh, and Jeffrey Parker.
Description: New York, NY : Routledge, 2021. | Includes bibliographical
      references and index.
Identifiers: LCCN 2020049249 (print) | LCCN 2020049250 (ebook) |
      ISBN 9780367343767 (hardback) | ISBN 9780367343774
      (paperback) | ISBN 9780429325373 (ebook)
Subjects: LCSH: Voice culture. | Acting. | Knight-Thompson
      speechwork.
Classification: LCC PN2071.S65 C33 2021 (print) | LCC PN2071.S65
      (ebook) | DDC 792.02/8—dc23
LC record available at https://lccn.loc.gov/2020049249
LC ebook record available at https://lccn.loc.gov/2020049250

ISBN: 978-0-367-34376-7 (hbk)
ISBN: 978-0-367-34377-4 (pbk)
ISBN: 978-0-429-32537-3 (ebk)

Typeset in Adobe Caslon Pro
by Apex CoVantage, LLC

For our students

CONTENTS

ACKNOWLEDGMENTS

This book would not exist without Knight-Thompson Speechwork®, nor its core text *Speaking With Skill: An Introduction to Knight-Thompson Speechwork* by Dudley Knight.

Who Are Knight and Thompson?

Dudley Knight (1939–2013) was a renowned actor, dialect coach, and voice teacher perhaps best known for his deep investigations into how speech methodology could most effectively be taught to actors. His articles *Standards* (*The Voice and Speech Review*) and *Standard Speech: The Ongoing Debate* (*The Vocal Vision*) illuminated and challenged the concept of speech training based on a prescribed speech pattern, and his book *Speaking with Skill* provided a comprehensive roadmap for skills-based speech pedagogy. Dudley spent a significant part of his career as a professor of drama at the University of California, Irvine, where he first encountered his eventual pedagogical partner, Philip Thompson, as a student during the 1980s.

Phil followed in Dudley's footsteps upon graduating—acting in and coaching plays across the country. While Head of Acting at The Ohio State University, Phil began to develop teaching and coaching strategies inspired by the techniques he had learned from Dudley. Phil returned to UC Irvine in 2001 to work alongside Dudley Knight as a faculty member, whereupon he discovered that the two of them had made similar discoveries and strides in their speech training research.

Together they worked to expand, explore, and refine their nascent method. They began offering workshops to other teachers in 2002 and in 2012 offered their first Teacher Certification course in their newly minted technique: Knight-Thompson Speechwork (KTS). Both Dudley Knight and Phil Thompson have been nationally renowned teachers and coaches, Master Teachers of Fitzmaurice Voicework®, former Presidents of the Voice and Speech Trainers Association, Full Professors at UC Irvine, published authors with several excellent articles in *The Voice and Speech Review*, and brilliant, inspiring teachers.

Who Are We?

We, the authors, were fortunate enough to study under both Dudley and Phil and have spent our academic careers exploring how to best teach the skills, knowledge, and values of KTS to students, actors, and teachers around the world. It is impossible to overstate the value of Dudley's work, just as it is impossible to adequately and accurately describe Dudley's brilliance, warmth, wit, and generosity. It is our highest and greatest intent that this book honors his person, his teachings, and his legacy.

As such, this book is not designed as a replacement of or an improvement on *Speaking With Skill*. Rather, *Experiencing Speech* is a text that can serve as either a companion piece or an introductory on-ramp to *Speaking With Skill* and, more broadly, Knight-Thompson Speechwork.

Who Shapes This Work?

One of the key tenets of KTS is the continual charge to investigate, to question, and to explore speech training methodologies that reflect the world in which we live. To quote Dudley,

> Whether they are called techniques, systems, approaches, methods, explorations, or any other label, and whether their practitioners admit it or not, anything we teach in the arts is based on some set of underlying propositions. If these propositions are examined regularly, poked at occasionally to enliven them,

soundly thrashed if required, rearranged when necessary, dusted off, polished, and generally looked after, the owner can offer them . . . to the partaker as principles. If they are neglected or ignored, they will gradually atrophy into inert assumptions.

(Speaking With Skill, ix)

Inspired by this charge from Dudley, the KTS community is currently (and perpetually) engaged in conversations about how to refine, adapt, clarify, and communicate speech skills to actors, to students, and to audiences. It is this community and this conversation that moves our system forward.

We offer special thanks to the Borchard Foundation for the grant and residency which supported the writing of this work. For Phil's generous contributions to this text, and for Erik Singer and Tyler Seiple's invaluable contributions to how we teach this work, thank you. We thank our teacher, Catherine Fitzmaurice, whose precept to "teach the person in front of you" inspires all of our teaching.

Last, but certainly not least, we'd like to express our deepest gratitude and appreciation for our KTS community: it is through our work together that KTS advances, thrives, and reflects the mission of socially aware, effective, comprehensive speech training. So, to all of our past, present, and future KTS teachers/students/actors/friends, thank you.

PREFACE

What follows is an introductory skills-based approach to speechwork for the actor. These skills can be applied to any circumstance in order to create a pronunciation pattern appropriate for any particular context. In laying out this approach, we have defined a set of guidelines designed to be challenged from time to time by you, the user of this text. Here are our Principles (perhaps) or Precepts (possibly). Do you agree?

1. Everyone has an accent. No one's speech is "neutral" or "general."
2. There is no good or bad way to speak. There is only what is good (or bad) *for* a particular context. Speech itself has no inherent qualities that could be assessed as good or bad. You may *prefer* one accent or pattern to another, and that's fine. Having preferences is human.
3. All humans have preferences. Whether conscious or not, preferences can become prejudices against or in favor of a group of people if separated from our sense of fairness. At this point they become biases. Perhaps we can't ever fully free ourselves from our biases, but being aware of our biases is essential so as not to inadvertently weaponize them.
4. The only baseline "standard" our role as storytellers requires is being understood (unless obfuscation is the goal). But

intelligibility is a moving mark based on your target audience. It is not one truth held by one person or persons (including the authors of this speech text!). Intelligibility is about communication, and communication is both giving and receiving. It is a relationship between speaker and listener. Whatever skills we deploy in our speech must be guided by the changing needs for communication within that relationship.

5. Speech training is an essential and deeply integrated layer of actor training, and as such it is part of a complex and subtle developmental process. As with all parts of actor training, the development of skills is not arrived at mechanically or by rote, but by cultivation and play, and by an incremental deepening of experience.

6. A skills-based approach to speech training invites the actor to explore all skills, not merely those that have been marked as socially preferred. Limiting the opportunity to play with the full range of possible speech sounds is impoverishing to the imagination. This work trains actors in the practice of expanding expressive territory through speech.

7. Even though this text is originally being written in English, the work within begins with an exploration of the fundamentals of human language. It represents a universal approach which can be applied to any spoken language. We hope to see this work taken up across languages and cultures, translated, and continually reimagined as a panlingual approach.

TEACHER INTRODUCTION

Welcome to *Experiencing Speech*! Thank you for adopting this text for your speech course.

How Does Knight-Thompson Speechwork Train Actors?

KTS, through rigorous play and experiential exploration, offers actors a wealth of speech and accent skills that enable them to make and identify every sound in every language on the planet and that empower them with the sensitivity and agency to make a full range of vocal choices based on their personal and performative circumstances.

How Can This Text Support Teachers?

As our teacher Dudley said in his text *Speaking With Skill*, this work "attempts to stay true to the actual, practical needs of the actor as distinct from applying a system based on the convenience of the teacher" (Knight, ix). Our goal is to inspire students' interrogation of speech actions, sounds, and uses. You, as a teacher of this work, may not be able to anticipate the breadth and depth of your students' inquiries, and you may not have all the answers they seek. Therefore, teaching this work will not always feel comfortable. A teacher must venture into territory that may not be fully known, but this adventurous spirit is excellent modelling for our students who we ask to courageously enter into the unknowns of the acting task.

Acknowledging that this work is not simple or easy to teach from the text alone, we want this text, and our supplemental teaching materials housed at https://es.ktspeechwork.org, password "Omnia", to support your classroom planning as much as possible. Throughout this text you will see website icons like the one in Figure 0.1 guiding you to various web resources including video examples of exercises, audio recordings of modeled sounds, and printable placards to use in your classroom.

Figure 0.1 Website Icon

How Does This Text Relate to *Speaking With Skill?*

Dudley's text was designed with the framework of a graduate school acting program or conservatory training program in mind—a program in which students and teachers have the luxury of speech class for multiple terms in sequence. However, many undergraduate theatre programs, private courses, and MFA programs do not share that same curricular real estate. In such instances, students and teachers may have only one term available to explore and develop speech skills. Hence, this text is modeled on a 16-week term that seeks to establish a foundation of speech skills prior to the complex task of performing in accent. Those working outside of the academic structure will find that they can work through this text at their own pace. If presented within an academic structure, this text is designed to encourage a two-term sequence whereby students work through this text, *Experiencing Speech*, in one semester, followed by a semester of experiencing accents.

Additionally, this text differs from *Speaking With Skill* in that it does not focus on American English as the target language and speech configuration for students. Rather, it focuses more broadly on speech skills which can be applied to any language context.

Does This Text Teach a Standard Pronunciation Pattern?

There are many names for standard pronunciation patterns taught in actor-training programs: *Standard, General, Neutral, Non-Regional, Stage*

Standard, or *Broadcast Standard.* Or, in terms of U.S.-based training programs, *Mid-Atlantic* or *Good American Speech.*

Because KTS as a pedagogy takes a *de*scriptive (rather than a *pre*scriptive) approach to speech training, it does not include teaching a standard pronunciation pattern of any kind, for any language.

If This Text Doesn't Teach a Standard, What Does It Teach?

This text teaches isolation skills, anatomy, and the physical actions of the vocal tract (*all* of them) and how to apply these skills to create any pronunciation pattern needed for any circumstance.

Is This a Phonetics Textbook?

In the sense that the student of this text will learn the physical actions behind every symbol in the International Phonetic Alphabet, yes. But *that* is where the emphasis lies, not in the memorization and practice of writing the symbols of the International Phonetic Alphabet. The ability to make and describe these sounds is accentuated, rather than the ability to write them down in the shorthand developed by the International Phonetic Association. This isn't to say that this text will not utilize phonetics in analysis and transcription; it's merely to indicate that the focus is on what the symbols represent, not the symbols themselves. We encourage emphasis on transcribing sounds at the more advanced level of accent analysis, which is beyond the scope of this text.

Does This Text Apply Only to English?

No; the skills laid out in this text can apply to any accent of any language! You might even be reading this text in a language other than English. It's up to the speakers (and listeners) of a language to determine what articulations are intelligible, or sweet, or magical, or perfectly suited to the needs of the storyteller in that language. This text is about building the awareness and skill to understand and create those articulations; that process is universal and applicable to all languages.

Further, we encourage you, the teachers of this work, to invite and include in your classroom the expertise of all your multilingual students. All sounds are useful for the actor, and these students possess skills for sounds you may not possess. We see that as a valuable asset to this process of skill-building for the entire class. This active inclusion also serves to empower multilingual students to take ownership of their expertise. We have marked a few moments in the text where performing text in multiple languages will be useful. Be on the lookout for more moments.

Who Is This Text For?

While this text is made up of distinct modules imagining a 16-week progression, the amount of time spent in each module is flexible. This book can be adapted to serve the private coach, the conservatory setting, a combination voice/speech course, or any host of scenarios where the reader desires to enhance their awareness of speech skills.

As teachers of this text, you should feel empowered to move through the text at a pace that is best for you and your students. Just as the skills in this work are modular and rely on the actor's agency to make thoughtful choices for any given context, so, too, are the lessons themselves. You may find that one module can be sufficiently explored in a day, whereas your students may need more than a week to explore a different module.

What Is the Best Way to Use This Text?

The efficacy of this text is directly related to the curiosity, patience, playfulness, questioning, and generosity of the teachers and students. It may sound paradoxical, but releasing ourselves from the burden of immediate understanding and "getting it right" invites deeper, broader knowledge. We invite both you and your students to approach the work under a "veil of ignorance," forgetting what you know so that you may discover even more.

We encourage reflection and questioning throughout the work and have put the icon displayed in Figure 0.2 at various places where we have found students are in need of some collective processing. The locations of these reflection moments are merely our suggestions to you. Please feel free to engage in reflection whenever you have the impulse.

Playfulness not only makes speech class enjoyable but also serves to connect to the play-focused mindset that allowed us to acquire speech skills as children. So, our invitation to you is to lean into the playfulness whenever you find it appropriate.

Figure 0.2 Reflection Icon

At the end of most modules, you will find a list of vocabulary words under the heading "Terms for Your Knowledge Celebration." In addition to the specific homework assigned at the end of each module, the student's task is to meet with a partner for some low stakes quizzing . . . or Knowledge Celebration! It's a simple form of retrieval practice that we have found incredibly effective for turning what could be a forgotten vocabulary list into a functional lexicon for your classroom interrogations, discussion, and performance.

Additionally, we believe speechwork is acting work. Rather than focusing on *product*, this text encourages a *process* of exploration and play that mirrors processes taught in other acting courses and serves to integrate speech training into the whole of the acting task.

Be curious. Have fun. Encourage patience and give yourself permission to enjoy the puzzle, the curiosity, the "beginner's mind." We hope you find these methods and skills as enriching, informative, and empowering as we do.

STUDENT INTRODUCTION

Welcome to *Experiencing Speech*!

Why Do I Need a Speech Class When I Already Speak My Native Tongue With Unconscious Competence?

. . . you might ask? Actually, you've answered your own question with the word "unconscious." To be fair, *we* really asked the question, but you're hopefully getting the gist of how this text will speak with you. Our goal is to help you make your speech choices within the acting task a *conscious* exploration as you find the choices that fit for any particular speech context. You might make one set of choices if you're in a contemporary play, another if you're voicing a fantasy character for a video game, and perhaps yet another if you're performing in an outdoor Shakespeare festival. Those are just three examples—there are *countless* more in the life and work of an actor. All these contexts ask different skills of you. And because your speech choices are a subset of your acting choices, approaching each of these three types of roles with the same default speech choices would be limiting your expressive territory. Or, conversely, trying to make different speech choices for those three roles without the skills to fully integrate them into your performance might result in some excellent final consonants, but also some lost humanity. We want this text to help *expand* your expressive territory and give you all the skills necessary to make specific speech choices integrated into your overall acting choices for *any* text! So speechwork isn't a thing that is added at the end of your rehearsal process solely for the purpose of reaching the back of the theater. It's another skill to help you play the action of your text!

When Do We Get to Do Accents?

This book covers the skill-building required *before* adding the complex acting task of learning and integrating accents into a performance. Before we get to *integrating*, we need to get to *interrogating*.

Some things to consider: What are your default speech choices? Or even more simply, what is speech? In this text we will ask you to examine speech from a place of conscious curiosity, one step at a time along the path to building language. We invite you to explore the exercises under a *veil of ignorance*—meaning, please forget what you know. Fight the impulse to draw conclusions or seek simple answers. Stay in the exploration and curiosity, as you likely did the first time you learned a language.

Is This the Class About All Those Weird Phonetic Symbols?

Good question! Yes and no. Yes, in that we will be exploring phonetics throughout this text. No, in that this course is not about phonetic *symbols*. It's about language and how we use it! Sometimes it will be important to get specific about how we refer to speech actions in language, and so we turn to phonetic symbols as *one tool* for that purpose. But we will use only some of our time together exploring the actual symbols that represent the speech actions we play with. Phonetic symbols will become much more significant when we take on the more complex goal of acting in accent. Again, this text will prepare you *up until* that point.

Will I Learn How to Speak Correctly in This Class?

Nope. Release the notion that "correct" is a thing that is real when it comes to speech. It's not.

How Am I Supposed to Do That?

Do all the exercises in the book. Give yourself permission to play! Experience! Be curious!

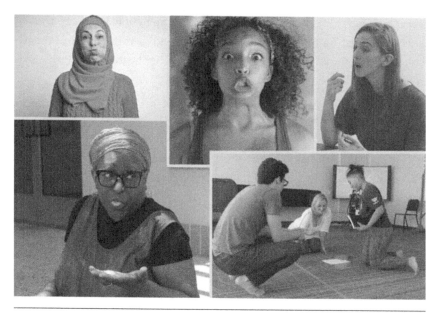

Figure 0.3 Speechwork in Action

PART ONE
THE PHYSICAL ACTIONS OF SPEECH

Module One
Experiencing Flow

Do you have your veil of ignorance on? Are you willing to forget what you know about language? This is our project. Coming to this project with fresh eyes, ears, mouths, and hearts will reap benefits beyond your imagination. Are you ready?

On our path toward language, let's start with the first step.

What Is Sound?

To state it over-simply: **sound** is a type of energy produced by vibration. When an object vibrates, it causes movement in the air particles, creating sound waves. A bat striking a ball creates sound waves, as does a raindrop striking the ground, as does a tree falling in the forest. These sound waves travel through the air, flowing in an undulating pattern, until eventually the energy that created the wave dissipates and the sound fades into silence.

While it's possible to perceive sound waves in other ways, the primary mechanism that hearing individuals use to interpret sound is the ears. Sound waves strike the ears and enter the ear canal, hit the eardrum and three very tiny bones (hammer, anvil, stirrup) and a tiny seashell-shaped repository filled with fluid and hairs (cochlea), before meeting the auditory nerve and sending those sound signals to the brain as information that can be understood and processed. A complicated procedure, but one

Figure 1.1 Sound Waves Become Meaning

that occurs almost all the time, and at an astonishing rate of speed! Simply put, sound waves enter your body where they are interpreted into meaning.

For hearing individuals, sound is a key means of experiencing the world. The booms, pops, crackles, and other periodic interruptions of air flow can be shaped into sounds that carry important intellectual and emotional information. From the sound of a sizzling skillet to air conditioner rattles to elevator music, sound is a constant presence in our lives. It's very likely that your lives have had a personal soundtrack as far back as you remember. Your ears and brains are so remarkably developed that you can pick up a great deal of information from a variety of sources. If prompted, you could recall and describe a number of meaningful sounds from your past, or even describe any number of sounds occurring at present. Let's begin there.

Exercise 1: Experiencing Sounds Occurring Right Now

If you feel comfortable doing so, close your eyes so you may suppress visual information for a moment. Let your attention be in this room, within these four walls. What do you hear? For now, keep your observations to yourself, but interrogate the sounds in the room, rather than labeling them by their sources. For instance, you might hear something you could identify as the heating or cooling system. But before you reach the conclusion, "That's the A/C!" try to describe the actual sounds it's making. Be creative in how you describe them. Do you hear a whirring? A rattle? A high-pitched hum?

After you've listened to the room, keep your eyes closed and expand your attention to include other parts of the building. What do you hear?

After you've listened to the building, expand your attention to include outside the building. What do you hear?

Then come back to the room again. What do you hear now?

Open your eyes.

Reflection

Can you describe your experience of that exercise?

Just as all of these sounds are shaping your current experience, an actor's voice shapes the experience of an audience. The voice is a remarkably complex and powerful *instrument* capable of flexibility and fluidity. That's right: your voice is an instrument.

Do you mean my voice is literally an instrument, or are you just being metaphorical?

It's really an instrument! Every musical instrument (including your voice) has similar components: **a power source** (something that initiates), an **oscillator** (something that vibrates), and a **modifier** (something that shapes the sound).

For example, a piano:

- The power source is the initiating energy of the finger striking a key, which causes a hammer to then strike one of the 88 strings.
- The oscillators are the strings that vibrate.
- The varying lengths of the strings are the modifiers that produce different frequencies of sound, which we perceive as pitches.

Okay, what is the power source for the voice?

Good question! It's the flow of your breath. We will refer to it as the **flow** for short.

Figure 1.2 Katie S's Vocal Tract

What is the oscillator, or the thing that vibrates?

The **vocal folds,** sometimes called the vocal cords. These folds are located in your voice box.

What is the modifier, or the thing that shapes the flow of sound?

The **vocal tract**—the flexible tube that is the distance between your lips and nose and your voice box. Take a look at this student's vocal tract. Their name is Katie S!

In music, the modifier shapes flow into a wide variety of pitches. In vocal communication, our vocal tract shapes flow into a wide variety of sounds that we call . . . wait for it . . . *speech.* That wide variety of vocal tract shapes is what this text is focused on.

What makes up the vocal tract?

Muscles! Also some bone, connective tissue like cartilage and tendons, and mucous membrane. A wonderful way to consciously interocept (or *sense the inside*) of the vocal tract is to track the journey of breath.

Your Three AAA's

You have *A*utonomy, *A*gency, and the *A*bility to choose your level of engagement in this work. We will ask you to explore various inquiries, exercises, and experiments within this text designed to test the boundaries of your comfort. It's up to you to decide when you've hit a boundary you're not able or willing to cross. These boundaries may shift throughout the training process of an actor, and certainly throughout the lifetime of an actor. So, you may want to revisit a boundary from time to time that previously felt fixed or immovable. You may not agree with your past self's boundaries!

Exercise 2: Experiencing the Flow of Breath

Check in with your body. Make any adjustments you might need to be more comfortable.

Begin with your eyes closed and your jaw relaxed open. Find some length in your spine; let your tailbone drop and your head and neck float upwards.

Take a moment to notice what you notice. Bring your thoughts into the room, in this moment. Then consciously turn your thoughts towards observing your breath.

After a moment you may note that you don't have to "take" a breath, or actively suck in air—your body knows how to breathe perfectly well without your conscious control. Observe your breath's involuntary rhythm. Feel which parts of your body rise and fall. And notice whether your inhalation and exhalation create noise or are essentially silent.

Explore what adjustments you might make with your body to make more sound with your breath. How much effort are you using to make more sound with your breath? What is the least amount of effort you need to make more sound?

Then, let your breath be silent. Notice what adjustments you may have made to arrive at that silent breath.

Where are the ports of entry for your breath? Is breath entering through your mouth? Your nose? Both?

If your mouth is open, try closing it and breathing in and out ONLY through your nose. Feel that the flow is most likely cooler as you breathe in and warmer as you breathe out (unless your environment is significantly hotter than your body temperature). Tune into the cooler sensation to track the breath's journey into your nostrils and down into your throat. After breathing through your nose for a few breath cycles, let your lips part so you can breathe through your mouth. See if you can breathe

ONLY through your mouth. Do you need to plug your nose to do so? Or can you figure out another way?

Again, use the air temperature to observe the sensation of the breath through the vocal tract. Then, take some time going back and forth between breathing only through your nose and only through your mouth. How are they different? Now, try breathing through both your mouth and nose at the same time. Can you do it?

 Reflection

Some things to consider: What might you engage to change the breath's port of entry? Does the breath move faster through the nose, or the mouth? Does one feel more comfortable for you than the other? Do you have a preference? Was your breath silent as you were exploring the different ports of entry? Or was there some sound?

Exercise 3: Increasing the Flow

In the last exercise, we encouraged you to let the breath be involuntary and silent. Now let's see what happens if you increase the breath flow.

In your relaxed, comfortable, easy breathing position, start to draw in more air on the inhalation and release more on the exhalation. Did you change anything about your mouth or throat? If so, what? Can you increase the airflow without changing anything in the mouth and throat or tensing anything up?

Is that even possible?

Yes. Your first impulse may be to work from a place of strength or force. However, with practice you will be able to focus the effort where it needs to be (in this case pressure from the lungs) and let everything else (vocal tract, shoulders, chest, etc.) relax. In fact, masterful speechwork requires such a sophisticated balance of effort and release, rather than a great degree of muscularity. It can take a few minutes, hours, days (lifetimes?) of playing with an exercise to find the somatic pathways to achieve that balance.

Go back to experimenting with increasing the breath flow. If you begin to get light-headed, or feel an uncomfortable pressure in your throat, have a rest.

As you increase your breath flow, your breath might start to make sound. We could describe that sound as "heavy breathing," or something akin to the breathing patterns of Darth Vader (you know, from *Star Wars*). For our purposes, we'll refer to this as **noisy breath**. Noisy breath occurs when the amount of air flow is larger and faster than the vocal tract can accommodate. The air bounces off the surfaces of the tract to create the sound.

I can hear noisy breath coming out and going in. Is that supposed to happen?

You just proved it's physically possible! Take a moment to explore noisy breath on both the exhalation and the inhalation. Breath going out is **egressive**, and breath coming in is **ingressive**.

Exercise 4: Testing the Breath—Is It Language?

Get a partner and have a conversation about something you're grateful for, using only noisy breath.

 Reflection

How did that go? Have we arrived at our destination: language? If not, what else do we need?

What did this, and the other exercises, reveal to you about the breath? Discuss this question within the group before settling on any specific answers.

Here are a few things this exercise may have revealed:

- Breathing occurs almost constantly, and it is usually silent.
- Breathing continues its flow without any conscious will, but we can also control the flow, deciding when and how we breathe.

- Air moving through a tube (like the vocal tract) doesn't create a lot of sound, unless the air is moving quickly.
- We can create noise whether breathing ingressively (inhaling) or egressively (exhaling).
- It would be very limiting to communicate to other humans if controlling the hiss and noise from our breath stream were the *only* ways to make sound. We need more tools to create sound! We need voice!

Great! We've got our power source—the flow of breath—and the tube that can modify that flow—the vocal tract. Now we need our oscillator—the vocal folds! While you may have heard them referred to as vocal cords, it's perhaps more accurate to call them folds, as they are actually two folds of flesh rather than a pair of strings.

Imagine that you're an alien anthropologist discovering a human neck for the first time. Place your fingers on your throat and investigate the shapes and textures you feel there.

As you explore, you might notice a slightly hard protrusion in the front of the throat, floating near-center. You've just found part of your **larynx**, which is the anatomical name for the aforementioned voice box.

Is that my Adam's Apple?

It could be! Or your Eve's apple! Different bodies will be shaped differently, and gendering those shapes may not always be useful (or appropriate). Let's call it your laryngeal shield.

All Bodies Are Different

The first anatomical image we introduced in this text a few pages ago depicts one possible version of a head, neck, and vocal tract. It may not look like your head, neck, and vocal tract, and that's okay. All bodies are different. We want you, the reader, to learn about your own anatomy free from judgment about what is good or right or correct. Seeing an anatomical image, and discovering that one's own anatomy may not align with said image, can tell a story that is not true. "I'm not like this image; therefore, my body is not ideal or correct." *Not. True.* We must keep in mind that anatomical images represent an *average* of many bodies but *not* a standard or correct body. Remember this as we introduce more anatomical images. Your uniqueness is what we celebrate—not your conformity.

Web Resource 1: Model Larynx

In your web resources, you'll find instructions on how to build a model larynx from paper and even how to crochet your very own larynx. We could spend a great deal of time exploring the various laryngeal components and how they all fit together. For our purposes, let's focus on two primary components: the **thyroid cartilage** and the **arytenoid cartilages**.

The protrusion you feel at the front of the throat is the thyroid cartilage. This shield-like structure not only protects your windpipe but also provides an anchoring point for the vocal folds.

The vocal folds meet in the back of the windpipe and can come together or apart thanks to the arytenoid cartilages.

How do the arytenoids bring the vocal folds together?

To explore this, clap your hands.

More precisely, clap your hands together with your palms touching closely and your fingers extended away from your body. In this exploration, your hands represent a simple yet accurate model of the larynx. Your fingertips are oriented at the front of the neck, and the heels of your hands are oriented toward the back. More specifically, your fingertips represent the anchoring point of the vocal folds to the laryngeal shield, or thyroid cartilage.

Keeping your fingertips together, open the heels of your hands away from each other. They represent the arytenoid cartilages. They are the back of the vocal folds and control whether or not the vocal folds are apart (*abducted*) or together (*adducted*).

Now bring the heels of your hands together again. And apart. Together. Apart. This action represents the folds coming together and moving apart.

The vocal folds close and open the pathway of air flowing to or from the lungs. The name for that opening is the **glottis**. When the glottis is open, the air flows freely. When the glottis is closed, it doesn't. But there's another possibility: When we bring the folds together, we can make them flutter open and closed in a wave pattern. How quickly or slowly this pattern repeats, or the **frequency** of this pattern, determines the **pitch** of the speaker. A singer singing the pitch commonly identified as "concert A," or the "A" above middle "C," will have their vocal folds come together and flutter apart 440 times per second on that pitch! If the singer were to jump up an octave, the "A" in the higher octave would be produced by the folds coming together 880 times per second!

These are astonishingly high numbers. Were the vocal folds dependent only on their own energy to move, do you think they could oscillate that quickly? Is there any muscle in the body that can move 880 times a second?

No! So, if it's not a muscular action, what brings the vocal folds together and apart so fast?

It's the flow of breath itself!

One of the ways an airplane stays in the air is by generating "lift." That "lift" is caused by a pressure differential that results in the wing moving up. A similar process is occurring with our vocal folds. The air moving past the vocal folds creates an area of low pressure, sucking the folds together and briefly stopping the flow. This starts up an alternating pattern of opening and closing that creates the pressure waves we hear as voice.

We can use the muscles of the larynx to adjust the shape, position, and tautness of the vocal folds and the pressure of air flowing past them to create a wide range of vibrations. Think about the sound that a creaky door makes. Can you imitate that sound using only the flow of breath to bring your vocal folds together and then apart, over and over? If you can, you've found your way to a different kind of flow called **creak**. Creak is a relatively slow flow of breath through the vocal folds, causing them to oscillate at approximately 20–50 times per second. A heck of a lot slower than the 440 of "concert A!"

Web Resource 2: Creak audio

Is creak the same as "vocal fry"?

It's not! Vocal fry implies that there is some extra effort or squeezing in the muscles around the larynx. Creak happens without that extra effort or squeeze. If you're feeling tension as you creak, try gently moving your larynx from side to side with one hand.

Exercise 5A: Testing the Creak—In and Out?

Can you creak both ingressively (in) and egressively (out)?

Exercise 5B: Testing the Creak—Is It Language?

Find a partner and have a conversation about your dream role, using only creak.

How did that go? Have we arrived at our goal of achieving language yet?

Not sure. It's difficult to control breath for long phrases of creak. I want to use my regular voice!

Let's do it!

Exercise 6A: From Creak to Voice

Bring your hand to the front of your larynx and find some creak again. From there, increase the flow of your breath until you might start to hear something that sounds like regular voice—or full **phonation**. Do you feel vibrations under your fingertips at the front of your larynx? Does it feel different from the pulsing of creak?

Can you phonate both ingressively and egressively? Try it.

Exercise 6B: Testing Phonation—Is It Language?

Find a different partner. Conduct a debate on the greatest television show ever, using only phonation.

How did that go? Have we arrived at our goal of achieving language yet?

SILENT BREATH   NOISY BREATH   CREAK   FULL PHONATION

Figure 1.3 The Journey from Silence to Full Phonation

Exercise 7: Building a Classroom Larynx

Web Resource 3: Classroom Larynx Video and List of Materials

In order to deepen our experience, sometimes it's useful to follow up an internal exploration with a different vantage point and on a different scale. It's also a ton of fun. So, let's experience the function of the larynx on a larger-than-life scale!

You'll need two long, stretchy bands (ropes can work in a pinch) to act as the vocal folds. One person will be the Thyroid Cartilage, holding one end of each of the bands. Two people, representing the Arytenoid Cartilages, will each hold the other end of one of the vocal folds. The three people now form a "V" shape.

Now we need someone to represent Flow! That person sits beneath the "V"-shaped vocal folds and is the air flow from the lungs. Finally, we need two people to represent the oscillating action of the Vocal Folds themselves.

Exploring the steps toward full phonation:

1. The person representing Flow sends an arm gesture through the open vocal folds, or the glottis (the space between the vocal folds). If Flow is not too vigorous in their gesturing, the result will be largely silent. Everyone in the class, do this with your own larynx! Send silent flow through your glottis as you see it acted out in the laryngeal dance before you.

2. Flow now sends a more vigorous gesture up through the folds (remembering, of course, that the person representing Flow, being a person, is not *actually* made of air and therefore should practice caution so as not to break their classmates). We're at noisy breath! Remember, the flow is larger and faster than the vocal

tract can accommodate, so the result is some noise. Everyone in the class, do this as it's acted out!

3. Arytenoid One and Two now rock (or rotate; actor's choice) together to approximate (or bring together) the vocal folds. If a *slow* flow is sent through the folds while the folds are together, a reflexive oscillation occurs, too slow for regular voice. Vocal Folds One and Two, your job is to represent that oscillation as a slow undulation of the bands or ropes toward one another. We're at creak! Make some creak as you see it enacted! When the Classroom Larynx needs to inhale again, the Arytenoids must rock apart to open the folds and make space for air to come in the body. Repeat a few times.

4. If Flow increases the speed of their movement and Arytenoid One and Two rock together, Vocal Fold One and Two must undulate faster for full phonation. Class, try this transition from creak to voice as you see it enacted. Again, when the Classroom Larynx needs to inhale, the Arytenoids must rock apart to open the folds and make space for air to come in the body. Repeat a few times.

End of Module Wrap

You've experienced silent breath to noisy breath to creak to full voice. And, we haven't yet arrived at language! Why not? Get curious about what we need to get to language. Stick with that curiosity as you do the following homework assignments:

- Color in this familiar image (now with labels). As you color, experiment with different coloring techniques (shades, textures, etc.) to reinforce your experiential knowledge.
- Practice your ingressive and egressive noisy breath, creak, and phonation.

Knowledge Celebration

This is a learning strategy that emphasizes getting information *out*. You've just absorbed the information from this first module like a sponge. Now it's time to squeeze the sponge! In addition to the specific homework assigned at the end of each module, your task is to meet with a partner for some low-stakes quizzing—or Knowledge Celebration! We will list some terms to help focus your celebration. Your job is to ask your partner simple questions based on the terms. Questions like: "How many parts of the vocal tract anatomy can you name?" "Ingressive and Egressive: which one is air in, and which one is air out?" Have your books open! Refer to the lists! This is a low-stakes quiz after all. More of a celebration, really.

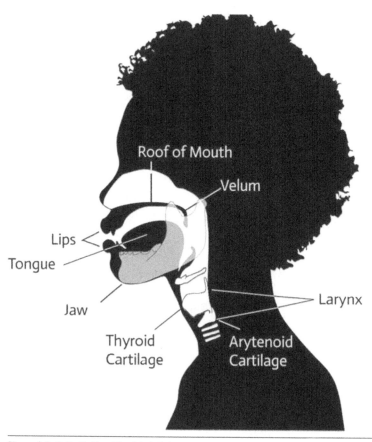

Figure 1.4 Katie S's Vocal Tract Labeled

Table 1.1 Terms for Your Module One Knowledge Celebration

VOCAL TRACT ANATOMY:	Sound
• Vocal folds	Oscillation
• Larynx	Phonation
• Thyroid Cartilage	Flow
• Arytenoid Cartilages	Noisy Breath
• Jaw	Creak
• Lips	Ingressive
• Tongue	Egressive
• Glottis	Frequency
	Pitch

MODULE TWO
EXPERIENCING ARTICULATORS

We've explored flow and identified it as the first and most important part of the sounds of human speech. We've also begun to explore the ways we can adjust that flow: to increase it, to interrupt it, to creak it, and to vibrate it.

Our next step will be to explore how we can make more and more complex variations in the flow as it moves through the rest of the vocal tract. To accomplish this, we'll need to identify and use more vocal tract muscles.

What Is the Function of a Muscle?

Simply put, a muscle exists to do one thing: contract. This contraction often has the byproduct of moving an associated bone, tendon, ligament, or other part of the body. When that muscular action is no longer necessary, the muscle releases. If you want to bring a dumbbell towards your shoulder, you'll likely activate and contract the muscles of the bicep. When it's time to return that dumbbell to its starting position, the bicep releases and a complementary muscle group takes over. Nearly every sound in every language is created by activating selected muscle groups to achieve a specific acoustic effect. Rather than lifting a dumbbell, you're lifting, advancing, curling, arching, cupping, protruding, raising, and lowering parts of the vocal tract to shape sound. You are so skilled at the muscular

Figure 2.1 Very Serious Gurns

actions necessary to create sounds in the languages you speak that you have developed "muscle memory" for them. But for an actor to experience and replicate *every* sound in *every* language, you'll need to develop muscular awareness and agility *beyond* your current patterns.

To accomplish this, you will need to develop a masterful, skillful practice in **gurning**. Gurning, of course, is the very serious art of making *very* funny faces.

Begin by moving the muscles in your face into any unique and vaguely hideous shape you can conceive. Please continue to breathe, but allow the flow to be silent. All facial and neck muscles are fair game in this exploration—get the forehead, the jaw, the eyebrows, the nostrils, and the neck all involved. Once you've found one particularly hideous configuration, begin to slowly morph into another, altogether different configuration. Move slowly, and explore!

Questions that may govern this exploration:

- Can you fit your entire face onto the tip of your nose?
- Can you fit your lips over your teeth?
- Can you squeeze every muscle towards your left eye?
- Can you move your mouth on a diagonal?
- Can you touch your earlobes with your lips?

Exercise 1A: Follow the (Gurn) Leader (If You Can)

Take turns making an athletic, creative gurn of your choosing, and see if the rest of the room can match your newfound face. Can you create a gurn so out there that no one can match it?

Exercise 1B: Mirrored Gurning

Find a partner to work with. One of you is A and one is B.

Choose a pocket of the room where you and your partner can comfortably face each other.

A will begin gurning slowly. B will attempt to "mirror" A's expressions perfectly. After a time, switch!

> A's role is not to trick B, but to move slowly and specifically enough that B can follow. You're both working together to create a mirror image. Also, remember to breathe! You can stay present to each other better when you allow (air) flow.

After you've done some gurning, how do your face muscles feel? It may feel like they've had a workout. We gurners are like athletes—though perhaps a better description of us might be "mouth-letes." If your muscles need a quick release, blow air out between your lips as if doing your best impression of a horse. It's likely you may have experienced a rapid fluttering of the lips. If you stick out your tongue and blow air out, you may be able to achieve a rapid fluttering of your tongue as well (if you were a rambunctious child, you may have some experience with this action). If you're not finding a flutter, you may need to experiment with increasing the airflow on the exhalation, and/or relaxing the lips and tongue.

The next step on our journey to language is to get more specific about naming and isolating the vocal tract muscles that shape gurns—because those vocal tract muscles also shape speech sounds! These muscles are called **articulators**. To begin, you will move them one muscle or muscle group at a time—in isolation—as a means of increasing the inventory of your gurn vocabulary and helping you on your way to becoming "mouth-letes."

Reflection

Get curious about which of your gurn-tastic muscles are going to have the biggest impact on shaping speech sounds. Discuss with a partner or group to see if you all agree.

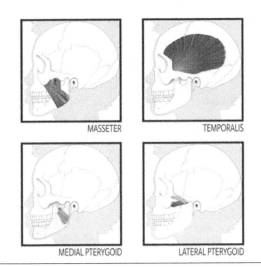

MASSETER TEMPORALIS

MEDIAL PTERYGOID LATERAL PTERYGOID

Figure 2.2 Jaw Muscles

The **Articulator Isolations** series is a way to develop the skills necessary to make every sound in every language. One can participate in articulator isolations while watching movies, lying in bed, commuting, or even writing chapters of a textbook.

Exercise 2A: Isolating the Jaw

Bring your fingertips to your **jaw hinge,** where your jaw neighbors your cheekbone. Briefly clench your jaw. Do you feel a muscle pop out? If you do, release your jaw and use your fingertips to massage into that muscle. That muscle is the **masseter** muscle, and it's the strongest muscle in the human body in terms of the ability to produce pure force. An average human has the bite capacity of about 200 pounds of force, and the world record for strongest bite is a whopping 975 pounds of force.

The masseter is one of three muscles that **raise** the jaw. When that muscle releases, the jaw likely **lowers** to a certain extent.

Next, bring your hands to your temples and slowly raise and lower your jaw. With your fingertips, feel the muscle that's working. That's your **temporalis**. It's the second of the three muscles that raise the jaw. Give your temporalis muscles a bit of a massage. Remember to breathe as you do so!

Before we massage the third muscle, make sure your hands are clean. Slide your right thumb inside your left cheek. Try to get your thumb even farther back than your back-most upper molar, up toward where your jawbone meets your cheek bone. Lightly pinch your cheek with your pointer finger on the outside and your thumb on the inside. Slowly raise and lower your jaw to feel the action of this muscle. Do you feel it working? If you do, massage it with your finger and thumb. Do the same on the other side. That's your **medial pterygoid**, and it completes the set of three muscles that raise the jaw.

You are most likely an expert at the muscular effort required to raise the jaw. You may find some practice will be necessary to become expert at doing the opposite—*releasing* those muscles.

Try This Expert Jaw Release

Tuck your thumbs into the place where your earlobes meet your skull. Let the palms of your hands rest on your jaw hinge, and let your fingertips fan up toward your temples. Slowly—at a glacial pace—keeping palms on face and thumbs tucked under your jawbone, let your thumbs trace the length of your jawbone down and then forward toward the point of your chin. Allow the hands to pull down slowly on the jaw muscles. Repeat as many times as you would like.

A Term of Art

This is "a word or phrase that has a precise, specialized meaning within a particular field or profession." "Expert Jaw Release" is the first of many Knight-Thompson Speechwork Terms of Art that will appear in this text. In your Knowledge Celebration tables at the end of each module, we will include a section for these KTS Terms of Art. They may not carry a lot of meaning outside our KTS universe, but they mean a lot for our journey within!

Another name for the jawbone, now blissfully relaxing away from your skull, is the **mandible**. We know it can raise and lower. If it couldn't, chewing food would be a most difficult proposition! It can also **advance**, bringing your lower front teeth more in line with your upper front teeth—or advance even further into an underbite. Try to isolate this jaw advancement and relax everything else. The muscle that advances the jaw is one we haven't massaged yet, and it's pretty difficult to feel from the outside. It's a pair of muscles called the **lateral pterygoids**. If we contract just one of the lateral pterygoids at a time—either the right or the left—we can move the jawbone from side to side. As you try that, again notice if you're using any other muscles that you don't need to.

The jawbone can also **retract**! Bring your jaw back to center if it's hanging out to one side, and then see if you can move your jawbone back, bringing your lower front teeth farther behind your upper front teeth.

Get Curious!

Part of our teaching philosophy is that an actor excited to learn more takes full ownership over their experience. We provide a foundation for your speech exploration within this text. We want you to want more! Be on the lookout for when your deeper curiosity strikes and give it what it wants. For example, if you're curious about the muscle that retracts the jaw, that's knowable information! Do some of your own research. *Speaking With Skill* and the web resources for this text are great places to begin your quest. Then connect that research back to an experience of your anatomy.

Now we know that the jaw can do multiple things. It can:

- Raise
- Lower
- Advance
- Retract
- **Move laterally**

Take a moment to return to your gurning. How does this new information about the jaw movement change your gurn vocabulary?

Can you find three distinct, repeatable gurns that involve the jaw? Try putting those three gurns together in a sequence, flowing from one into the other. We will revisit them soon, so you may want to make note of them.

Exercise 2B: Isolating the Cheeks

Lightly bite the inside of your cheeks, pulling them in closer to your teeth to do your best impression of a fish. Release. Then, see if you can pull your cheeks in closer to your teeth without biting the insides.

Next, keep your mouth closed and try to exhale. Let the out-breath gather in your mouth and puff out your cheeks, like a chipmunk with its cheeks full of acorns. Then, imagine you have mouthwash in your mouth. Swish it around, letting it stretch out your cheeks. Make sure you "clean" your upper and lower molars on both sides.

We just worked a set of muscles that run from your jaw hinge under your cheekbones down to the corners of your mouth, and also up from the mandible. They're called the **buccinators**. Let's have a contest. Press your tongue tip into the inside of your cheek in an effort to push it as far away from the teeth as possible. At the same time, use the buccinators to resist that action. Which muscle group will win? Make sure you try both sides.

How do I know if I'm actually isolating the buccinators, or if other things are engaging as well?

Great question! While we recommend practicing your isolations initially without visual reinforcement, at certain points, it may be very useful for you to have access to either a small handheld mirror, or a cell phone with a front-facing camera.

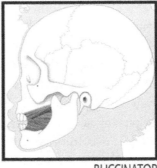

BUCCINATOR

Figure 2.3 Buccinator Muscle

Now we know that the cheek muscles can do a few things. They can:

- **Tense**, pulling the cheeks in against the teeth
- Relax
- And when they're relaxed, they can be stretched as the cheeks are puffed out away from the teeth

After exploring the jaw, we asked you to find three, distinct, repeatable gurns that flow into each other, creating a sequence. Can you now explore three more distinct, repeatable gurns that involve the cheeks and put them together into a sequence of six gurns?

Exercise 2C: Isolating the Lips

There are two concentric circles of muscle around the lips. Together, they are the **orbicularis oris**. Each ring of muscle can change the shape of the lips in different ways when we contract it. Let's start with the outer ring, which is outside of what we think of as our actual lips. Imagine a string attached to each of your lip corners. Pull the imaginary strings forward, bringing your lip corners along with them. Make sure the effort is just in your lip corners. When we **protrude** only our lip corners, we're engaging the outer ring of the orbicularis oris.

What if you did some extreme lip corner protrusion, to the point where your lips were pulled entirely away from your front teeth? Congratulations! You're **trumpeting** your lips. By contracting the outer ring of the orbicularis oris, we squish our lips towards the center of the circle, and they extend forward. That's a different sort of action than we've seen so far. Try that a couple of times—toggling back and forth between effort and release.

Now, let's engage the inner ring of the orbicularis oris—the muscle we think of as our actual lips. Bring your lips together so that they're touching and maybe even pressing into each other. Now you're **pursing** your lips. Relax that pursing action, and then bring your lips closer together without touching. This is still pursing! Try going from relaxed lips to pressing them together to just bringing them closer to each other a few times, in any order you like.

What if you pursed your lips, without letting them touch each other, to the point that your lips began to **curl** behind your front teeth and into your mouth? This is extreme pursing, or curling! Think back to that outer ring, and you'll feel that it is relaxing and stretching as the pursing action of the inner ring pulls the lips inwards.

If you engage both rings of the orbicularis oris at the same time, you'll have achieved **full lip rounding**. Try it! Protrude your lip corners. Now add pursing to the center of your lips. If you keep the corners protruded and alternate between pursing and relaxing the center of the lips, you can take your impersonation of a fish to the next level!

Extra Challenge: Try trumpeting or curling one lip at a time. Start with both lips relaxed. Trumpet just your top lip, keeping your bottom lip relaxed. Then trumpet your bottom lip, so that both lips are trumpeted. Then curl just your top lip, leaving your bottom lip trumpeted. Then curl your bottom lip so that both lips are curled. Repeat the cycle as many times as necessary until you are a master.

If your lips feel fatigued, take a short break before continuing. Really rest, though, because we have more work to do with the lips before we're done! In addition to the orbicularis oris, there are some other muscles that start at the lip corners and radiate out to the sides of the face like the hands of a clock.

Think about a reason to *smile* today and go ahead and smile! You just engaged one of these muscles. It runs from the lip corners up to your cheekbones, and it's called the **zygomaticus**. Try alternating between smiling and relaxing your lips completely—and make sure you're not using any other muscles or moving anything else!

Next, let's try a "creepy" smile. Instead of your lip corners traveling up toward your cheekbones, bring your lip corners straight back toward your ear lobes, so that your lips make a straight line. Use a mirror if that's helpful. The muscle making this creepy smile possible is the **risorius**. It **retracts** the lip corners straight back.

Sidebar

Many of these actions can be done one-sided! Try retracting just one of your lip corners towards the corresponding ear lobe. Then protrude the other lip corner. Take a look in a mirror to behold the glory of your new creation!

Now we know that the lips can do a lot of isolated actions. Those actions are:

- Lip corner protrusion
- Lip corner retraction—a.k.a. "creepy" smile
- Pursing
- Curling
- Trumpeting
- Full lip rounding
- Smiling

Give yourself two minutes to explore the gurns you can achieve using this newfound information about the muscles of the lips.

Choose your three favorite lip-based gurns and add them to your sequence of jaw and cheek gurns.

Exercise 2D: Isolating the Tongue

Because of the sheer flexibility of the tongue and its importance in speech actions, it will be helpful to identify different parts of the outside surface of the tongue before exploring its movements. To feel these different parts, you will need access to a mirror and something you feel comfortable touching your tongue with—like a clean fork, straw, or chopstick.

Take a moment to look at your tongue in the mirror. Can you observe it without judgment? Notice any differences in color and texture across the surface of your tongue. If your neighbor is feeling bold, perhaps they will allow you to look at their tongue, too! If so, notice any differences and similarities.

Return to observing your own tongue in the mirror. Bring your fork (straw or chopstick) to the very **tip** of your tongue—the edge at the very front of your tongue. Move your fork back and forth a bit to awaken some sensation there. Then, bring your fork a little farther back from the tip of your tongue, onto the front part of the top surface of your tongue. This area might differ in color or texture from the rest of the top surface. You might notice a difference in the appearance of the taste buds. You might even see a horizontal crease separating the front part of the top surface from the rest of your tongue. This is the **blade** of your tongue.

Then, bring your fork a little bit back from the blade of your tongue, still on the top surface. The rest of the top surface that we can see is the **body** of the tongue. We can divide the body into three parts: the **front**, the **middle**, and the **back**. Use your fork to explore the body, but take it only as far back as you feel comfortable.

Is the blade the same as the front of the body of the tongue?

It's not! The blade is in *front* of the **front**. When we talk about the front of the body, it's behind the blade.

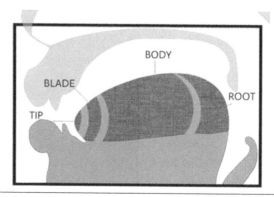

Figure 2.4 The Parts of the Tongue

What is that line that runs from the back of my tongue down to the tip,
right in the middle?

That's the **midline** of the tongue. With permission, investigate how yours might compare to your neighbor's.

Lastly, run your fork along the **side edges** of your tongue. Awaken some sensation there. You can also use your molars to lightly bite the side edges of your tongue.

Now that you've mapped out some tongue territory, move it! Start by sticking your tongue out! As far as you can! Then place a knuckle in that fleshy area under your chin and stretch your tongue out even farther. That fleshy area is the **root** of your tongue. It's important to note that the tongue is not just what we see when we open our mouths and look in the mirror. It goes all the way down to the larynx and can even be felt from the outside as you're doing now. Keep your knuckle under your chin and move your tongue back in your mouth. Do you feel any movement at the root? Keep bringing your tongue back in your mouth, as if your tongue was an accordion folding into the back of your throat. Any movement at the root?

With your knuckle still under your chin, stick your tongue back outside your mouth.

The movement you may be feeling is **tongue root advancement** and **tongue root retraction**.

Wait, the tongue root can move?

That's right! It can move in isolation from the rest of your tongue or in conjunction with it.

Next, stick your tongue outside of your mouth again. See if you can make your tongue skinny like a hot dog or like you're pointing at something with your tongue.

What if the side edges of my tongue curl up?

Then that's one of your special skills! For this exercise, though, see if you can pull the side edges of your tongue directly in towards the midline, rather than curling them up. When you make that hot dog tongue, you're **bunching** the tongue.

Keep your tongue outside of your mouth, and now spread it wide like a pancake. This is an active **spreading** and not a passive relaxation of the tongue! Reach those side edges out to make your tongue as wide as you can.

Go back and forth between hot dog tongue and pancake tongue a few times. Do you feel the burn, mouth-lete?

Onto the next tongue gurn! Stick your tongue out again, and then **curl** your tongue tip up towards your nose. Can you touch it? Then curl your tongue tip down towards your chin. Repeat those two actions a few times. Then reach the tip of your tongue to the left, and then the right. Repeat those two actions a few times.

Did you use your jaw in that exploration?

Try the exploration again, this time with a relaxed jaw. You might try resting your hands on either side of the jaw to prevent it from moving. Does that change or limit your tongue's range of motion? The more you can isolate the exploration to just the tongue, the more the tongue muscles will benefit.

With your tongue inside of your mouth, curl your tongue tip up to the roof of your mouth. Find the place where your upper front teeth meet your gums. Run your tongue tip along that spot for a bit. Then bring your tongue tip a little farther back on the roof of your mouth until you find a bump or a ridge. Run your tongue tip along that ridge—the **alveolar ridge**—and notice the texture(s) of it. Then bring your tongue tip a little behind that ridge to where you might feel a slope in the roof of your mouth. Run your tongue tip along that slope. You may find that area in particular has a lot of sensation when contacted. Lastly, bring your tongue tip farther back to where you may feel a hard dome-like or flat part of the roof of your mouth. This will likely take up most of the territory of the roof of your mouth and is your hard **palate**. Again, use your tongue tip to observe the texture(s) of that part of the roof. Continue the journey back until your tongue reaches a soft textured surface distinct from the palate. That area is the **velum**, sometimes called the soft palate. Take some time to investigate the texture(s) of the velum.

Let your tongue tip release back down and use your mirror to have a look at the roof of your mouth. A flashlight might be handy here. If you and your neighbor are comfortable with it, have a look at the roof of your neighbor's mouth. Are there similarities? Differences?

What if I'm not comfortable with that?

It sounds like you've found one of your limits. Know that there are limits that shouldn't be pushed. In our exploration, we should approach those limits consciously and listen with all our faculties to what our body is saying about our comfort level. Taking this investigation at a slow pace will leave more space for you to stop should you start to feel uncomfortable.

Back to the tongue! With your tongue inside your mouth, curl your tongue tip up to the alveolar ridge; then let it release down. Repeat a few times. Now bring the blade of your tongue to your alveolar ridge. Release and repeat a few times. Then curl your tongue tip up to your palate; let it release down. Repeat a few times.

Shift your focus now to the body of the tongue. With your tongue tip curled down inside your mouth behind your lower front teeth, stretch the front of the body of your tongue up towards your alveolar ridge. It might make contact, or it might not. You're **arching** the front of your tongue body. Let it release down so that your whole tongue body is flat in your mouth, as if your tongue body were the equator dividing the northern and southern hemispheres of your mouth. Repeat that action a few times. Then, keeping your tongue tip curled down, arch the middle of your tongue body up towards your palate. Again, it might make contact, or it might not. You're arching the middle of your tongue body. Try that action a few times. Lastly, keeping your tongue tip curled down, arch the back of your tongue body up to your velum. Try that a few times.

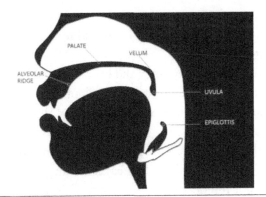

Figure 2.5 The Roof of the Mouth

What's the difference between curling and arching?

Curling is done with the tongue tip, and arching is done with the body of the tongue.

There is one more thing to do with the body of the tongue. Use the underside of the blade of your tongue to press down on the place where your lower front teeth meet the gums. Your tongue tip will probably curl up a little as a result. You'll then be making a kind of nest-shape in the front of your mouth where you might hold a blueberry or grape. You're **cupping** the front of the tongue body. Come back to your **Equator Tongue** (tongue flat in the mouth) and repeat that cupping action a few times. Then, use the underside of your tongue body to press down on the bottom of your mouth to create a nest-shape for that blueberry or grape in the middle of your tongue. You're cupping the middle of your tongue body. Try that action a few times. Lastly, see if you can create a cup in the back of your tongue body. Try that action a few times—without retracting your whole tongue!

Our last tongue gurn involves pressing the side edges of your tongue into the insides of your upper molars. You may feel that, to accomplish this, you are spreading your tongue like a pancake *inside* your mouth. That action is called **bracing** the tongue. Try that a few times.

We have a lot of possible actions for the tongue:

- Tongue root advancement
- Tongue root retraction
- Bunching the tongue (hot dog)
- Spreading the tongue (pancake)
- Curling the tongue tip up, down, and to the sides
- Equator Tongue
- Arching the front, middle, and back of the tongue body
- Cupping the front, middle, and back of the tongue body
- Bracing the side edges into the insides of the upper molars

Give yourself two minutes of gurn exploration with all of the various tongue movements described earlier. Can you guess what comes next? You've got it—develop at least three distinct gurns involving the tongue, and add them to your jaw, cheek, and lip sequences. You should be up to twelve sequential, repeatable, distinct gurns by the end of this exploration.

Exercise 2E: Isolating the Velum

The velum is a group of muscles that can **lift, lower,** and **spread**. You will probably feel it lift when you yawn—so, go ahead, yawn. (Yawning is a *skill* in speech class.) Do you feel it lifting and stretching?

Now add a tongue stretch to that yawn—what we call a **Professional Yawn**. Rather than letting your tongue retract, keep your tongue cupped in the bottom of your mouth, your tongue tip forward, and then stretch it outside of your mouth a bit. This is how cats and dogs yawn. Try it. Do you feel a stretch in your tongue root as well?

Can you yawn just from the right side of your velum (tip: it helps to reach up with the right arm at the same time)? How about on the left side? Now try both sides again, but without an arm reach.

Now try a **Master Yawn**. Yawn wide—straight out to the sides. Do you feel your velum spreading to the sides, flat like a pancake?

Next, bring the back of your tongue and your velum together, just as you did previously in the arching gurns. This time, intentionally make contact between the tongue and velum so that, even with your mouth open, any egressive phonation that you make would have to travel through your nose. You're lowering your velum to achieve that!

Figure 2.6 Animals Yawning Professionally

And so, the velum:

- Lifts
- Spreads
- Lowers

Return to the gurn sequence you've been crafting. Add two distinct gurns involving the velum. You should be up to fourteen sequential, repeatable, distinct gurns by now. Share them with the group!

I can practice some of the articulator isolations as you describe them.
Others I find more difficult to understand and do. Is there a place
I can go to find pictures of other people doing the isolations?

Yes! It was our intention that you try the isolations without a visual model at first. It's useful to experiment with your own proprioception (awareness of your body in space) and interoception (awareness of your body from the inside) before introducing external information, like from a mirror or picture.

In your web resources, there is an articulator isolations daily practice log that has photos of actors performing each isolation, along with more muscle descriptors for the speech geek's deep dive.

End of Module Wrap

Web Resource 4: Articulator Isolations Photos and Log

You have two homework assignments: one that is your new daily practice, and one that shall be a creative masterpiece of ridiculousness and skill.

- Practice the Articular Isolations daily! There is an Articulator Isolations log in your web resources that you can use to track your progress.
- Choreograph a "Gurn Dance" using the articulator isolations. Choose a piece of music that inspires you. Each articulator isolation should be used at least once.

Web Resource 5: Examples of Gurn Dances

- This is a *choreographed, rehearsed* Gurn Dance, not an improvisation exercise! You must be able to repeat your performance should you be called upon to teach it to the class.
- Refrain from using anything but your head and face for this exercise. No arms, no hands, no legs. You may perform this seated or standing up.
- Your dance should be as dance-like as possible in terms of rhythm, variety, and specificity.
- Make no noise whatsoever prior to, during, or at the end of your gurn dance. There should be no human voices whatsoever in the entire gurn dance. And ABSOLUTELY NO LIP SYNCING!
- Remember to breathe.

Table 2.1 Terms for Your Module Two Knowledge Celebration

JAW	TONGUE
• Masseter	• Tip
• Temporalis	• Blade
• Medial pterygoid	• Body (front, middle, back)
• Lateral pterygoid	• Midline
• Jaw hinge	• Side edges
• Mandible	• Root
CHEEKS	**ROOF OF MOUTH**
• Buccinators	• Alveolar Ridge
	• Palate
LIPS	• Velum
• Orbicularis oris (inner and outer rings)	
• Zygomaticus	**KTS TERMS OF ART**
• Risorius	• Equator Tongue
	• Expert Jaw Release
	• Professional Yawn
	• Master Yawn
	• Gurn

MODULE THREE
EXPERIENCING SHAPED FLOW

We are certain that your gurn choreography performances from the last module were at the same time masterful and outrageous. After practicing the articulator isolations, notice how much more detail and dexterity are available for your gurns. That's the masterful part of your work, because mastery makes room for both ease and precision. The outrageous part comes into play because you were willing to apply your studied and refined isolations to the reckless abandon of playing with gestures in your vocal tract. Let's get meta for a moment: this transition from deep investigation, interrogation, and isolation to audacious and adventurous application is a theme of our work together.

We will toggle *back and forth* between two states of learning throughout this text: **descriptive knowledge** and **embodied knowledge**. This is precisely the same process as the acting task: you read the script, do your research on the circumstances, learn your lines and your blocking, and then integrate everything you have discovered into the flow of the scene. You learn it, you integrate it, you do it. Remember when we said in the Principles (perhaps) or Precepts (possibly) that speechwork is a layer of actor training? You, dear actor, are becoming more skilled in your knowing *and* in your doing. Let's *do* a little to start off this module. Let's revisit your gurning.

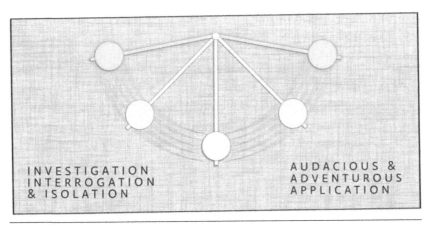

Figure 3.1 The Process Pendulum

Exercise 1A: Expert Gurning

Enter into an expert silent gurn session at a medium tempo. Notice your ability to find all the shapes you practiced in Module Two, paying particular attention, for *30 seconds each*, to the shapes you are able to make with the following articulators:

- Tongue
- Lips
- Velum

Exercise 1B: Expert Gurning—Adding Voice

Add voice to your gurn, but with this particular focus: notice the physical sensation of vocal tract shapes, and *then* notice the sounds that result from those shapes. In other words, instead of making sounds the goal, make vocal tract gestures the goal. Focus on moving the articulators and notice how the sounds change as a happy byproduct. This way, instead of being magnetized to familiar sounds, you may end up discovering sounds that are new, exciting, scary, ugly, beautiful, or ancient. Do this for a full minute without stopping (except, of course, to breathe and swallow as needed).

Exercise 1C: Expert Gurning—Noticing Vocal Tract Gesture Ripple Effect

Continue your expert gurning. Notice the physical sensation of vocal tract gestures. Notice the sounds that follow as a result, but also notice how those sounds make you feel. Which ones do you like making? Wonder why. Which ones do you not like making? Wonder why. If you come across a sound or a shape preference, great! That's one of your biases. Get familiar with your sound biases.

Wait, aren't biases bad?

They are harmless so long as you acknowledge them and note that they hold no inherent or universal value; they are simply your personal preferences. Notice if over time in the practice of this work those biases dissolve, change, or expand.

Exercise 1D: Expert Gurning—Move/Hold/Move

Return to your gurn. At a certain point in your gurn flow, hold your face in a particular shape. Send a flow of voice through that shape and notice what sound it makes. Now, breathe in to feel the cool air on your vocal tract. You may be able to feel more precisely the shape of your articulators with the sensation of cool air flowing in. Notice if it's a familiar shape or a new one. Also notice if you're being rigorous about keeping the same shape on the exhalation and the inhalation. Sometimes our mouths can have biases. Move again in your gurning for 30 seconds to a minute. Hold again in a shape. Make the sound of that shape. Breathe in. Notice. Repeat.

Continuing Our Path Toward Language

You may have noticed from the previous exploration that you are at times **shaping** the flow of voice, keeping *a certain amount of open space* between vocal tract surfaces, and at other times **obstructing** it, *bringing vocal tract surfaces into closer or full contact* with each other.

This is great! At this point on our path toward language, we *need* both shaping and obstructing! In Module One we explored the journey from silence to making our first vocal tract sounds by focusing on the power

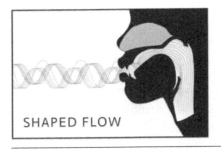
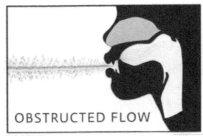

SHAPED FLOW   OBSTRUCTED FLOW

Figure 3.2 Shaping vs. Obstructing the Flow

source, or the flow of breath. You experienced the transition from silent breath to noisy breath to creak to full voice. Yet, without shaping or obstructing the flow, modifying only the type of flow was not enough to transform our efforts into a meaningful pattern we might recognize as language! In Module Two, we explored the ways in which articulators might move to shape or obstruct the flow. Yet, without different varieties of flow, those actions were not enough to get us to language. We need to combine varieties of flow with the actions of shaping and obstructing to get to language.

For this module, let's focus our exploring on shaping only. We'll explore lots of interesting ways to obstruct the flow in our next module.

Exercise 2A: Narrowing Your Expert Gurn Parameters

Start a gurn again, but with these limited parameters: focus your efforts on moving the lips (protrusion, retraction, pursing), the body of your tongue (arching and cupping, with the tongue tip largely not active, near the bottom teeth), and your velum (lifting and spreading). Be sure to keep enough space between surfaces in the mouth so that there is no obstruction at all! It may result in sounds that are more subtle—and that's okay.

Two reminders:

- As you explore, allow the rest of your face to relax. This exploration is just for the articulators mentioned earlier.
- Let the physical action lead and notice the sounds that result. Go for it.

What did you notice? Tell a friend.

Aren't we just making vowels?

Great question! What's a vowel? You may be able to answer this question using your *descriptive knowledge*. To discover an answer coming from your *embodied knowledge*, let's try the previous exploration again, but with this slightly modified prompt: make some vowels!

Exercise 2B: Narrowing Your Expert Gurn Parameters—Vowel Gurning

Thinking about only shaping vowel sounds with your articulators, enter into a gurn-a-thon. Explore how many vowels your gurning can create.

How did that go for you? Were you still letting the physical action lead and noticing the sounds that result from those shapes? Or were you magnetized toward sounds familiar to you? When you think of the idea of a vowel in your first language(s), what do you think of? As a native English speaker or a native Spanish speaker, for example, your brain might answer "AEIOU." That's a very limited set of sounds (and perhaps not the whole truth within those languages, at that). Hence, the term "vowel" has the potential to carry some unhelpful ideas about what is or isn't a useful shaped sound.

As an experiment, try to discover a new *shaped sound* that isn't part of your native tongue(s)! How would you describe the shaping of this new sound? Is there any way to describe it without referring to a known vowel sound?

As actors who eventually want to be able to embody characters with accent patterns different from your own, it's helpful to expand your understanding of what a vowel is. In acting class your instructor wants you to expand your expressive territory in terms of the actions you can play and the circumstances you can imagine and embody. Here in speech class, we want you to expand your expressive territory for the speech gestures you can make in your vocal tract, with the ease of a native speaker. And that takes practice, or *rehearsal*, if you will.

If the term "vowel" is limiting, can we just call these shaped, voiced sounds something else?

Absolutely. If we can agree on the goal of expanding expressive territory *and* we can agree that our idea of "vowel" may be unhelpfully limiting, then it's time we leave the term "vowel gurning" in favor of a more useful term. Let's borrow the Greek term for sound or voice ("phthongos") and use the term **phthong**. You may have heard this term before when describing two sounds, as in the term "diphthong," where "di" represents "two." We will define **phthonging** as **shaping the flow** of voice using the lips, tongue body (we will save the tip and blade for obstructing), and the velum.

Exercise 3A: Phthonging—An Introduction

With the term "phthong" we've broken out of the limitations of any particular language's vowels. That means that we can let our imaginations open up into *every* possible shape. Start slowly with micro-movements of the articulators. Let the physical action lead and notice the sounds that result. Notice how subtle a shift you can make and still detect a change in the sound. What is the smallest amount of effort needed to change phthong shape? How dramatically can you change the shape without obstructing the flow? How many gradations of shaped sound can you explore? Infinite phthongs!

Exercise 3B: Phthonging—A Maraphthong

Let your shape shifting begin to connect and flow into one long stream of phthonging. Guess what, mouth-lete, you have now entered into a *maraphthong*!

Exercise 3C: Phthonging—Sharing the Monophthong in Pairs

Find a partner and decide who is A and who is B. A will initiate a maraphthong with 15–20 seconds of uninterrupted phthonging. In the midst of this flow of phthong, settle on an interesting shape, and then hold that shape as you continue the sound. We will call this single phthong shape a **monophthong**. B, you should watch A closely and then precisely recreate the shape, and therefore the sound that A is making. A, you may need to offer some gentle feedback or guidance, using only your monophthong to communicate, of course. Find a way to agree when B has arrived at your shape. Then switch roles so B may be the phthong initiator. Repeat several times.

My partner's voice is a different pitch than mine so it's challenging to match their monophthong exactly. Is that okay?

That's absolutely fine! Because of the nature of human voice, your phthongs may be occurring in different pitch ranges. Speakers need not match pitch in order to match vowel shapes. In fact, it may be useful to uncouple those two features.

What are some observations you made while doing this exercise? Share with your partner.

It's easier for me to make my partner's shape and sound precisely when I'm looking into their mouth. Is that cheating?

Nope. You're using all the resources at your disposal. That's genius, actually. In addition to your listening with your ears to gather information, you're using your eyes to mirror the exact speech gesture your partner is making, or "listening with your eyes." This is very similar to how you learned your first language—not only did you mimic the *sounds* that adults were making for you, but you also mimicked the shapes which were most likely exaggerated and performed in a way to make it easier for you to copy.

But because we're phthong skill-building, it's also useful to *suppress* visual information to see how close we get to a shape *without* seeing.

Exercise 3D: Phthonging—Sharing the Monophthong Back to Back

Stick with your partner and, if back-to-back contact is permissible for both of you, touch backs. No contact is also fine. Now A will once again get a good maraphthong training session going, at least 15–20 seconds of phthonging. Then find a shape (with a sound associated) to freeze on and make that shape (and sound) for B. B, recreate the sound you're experiencing as precisely as possible. A, you may need to offer some gentle feedback or guidance, again using only your monophthong to communicate. When both of you feel you're making the same phthong, turn around to face each other. B can see how close they got to A's shape. If B is very different from A's shape, make A's shape using the added visual information. Then toggle between your previous shape and the new one.

Switch roles, so B may be the phthong initiator. Repeat several times.

With your partner, spend some time discussing your findings from this little experiment.

Getting It Wrong Is Getting It Right

When modeling someone else's speech sound, as in the back-to-back sharing in the monophthong exercise, "getting it wrong" is getting it right—meaning the process of deep investigation followed by performing a sound that is off from the target is an essential part of the learning process for becoming expert at speech sounds (and accent performance!). Being curious about "what went wrong" is just as important as being on target. In fact, this will help *the future you* hit that target, whatever it may be, with more accuracy, more consistency, and less fear. Keep this in mind and invite yourself to *practice without judgment*. Also, when giving feedback to your classmates on their speech sounds, remember to be gentle. Encourage a culture of practicing with curiosity.

Exercise 4A: Phongthing—Move/Hold/Move

Return to your solitary work in a familiar but slightly modified experiment. Enter into a maraphthong and hold in a particular shape. Send sound through the shape you're holding and continue to hold the shape steady. Now, breathe in to feel the cool air on your vocal tract so you may more precisely feel the shape of your articulators. Notice if it's a familiar shape or a new one for you. Move again in your phthonging for 30 seconds to a minute. Hold again in a shape. Make the sound of that shape. Breathe in. Notice. Repeat.

Exercise 4B: Phongthing—Move/Hold/Move—Lips Only

This is the same experiment as Exercise 4A but with one change: instead of holding both lips and tongue, hold the lips only and keep the tongue moving. Hold, breathe in, notice, and repeat.

Exercise 4C: Phongthing—Move/Hold/Move—Tongue Only

This is the same experiment as the previous two, but—you guessed it— instead of holding both lips and tongue, this time hold the tongue only and keep the lips moving. Hold, breathe in, notice, and repeat.

Exercise 4D: Phongthing—Move/Hold/Move—Velum Only

This one is a bonus round! Can you hold just the velum? What does it feel and sound like when you move the velum again? How does that movement change sound?

I can't move one articulator without another articulator moving as well!

If you find it challenging, you're most likely not alone! You may have found that your lips want to respond to your tongue movement, or vice versa, and so holding becomes challenging. Certain movements in your home-base musculature are likely coupled to one another. But if you're to fulfill your maximum potential as the dexterous mouth-letes we know you can be, we suggest you return to the Articulator Isolations from Module Two, and *often*. Remember that gurn sequence you crafted? Make a daily practice! Having the skills to decouple the movements of your tongue, lips, and velum from one another is at the heart of detailed speechwork (which can eventually support nuanced accent acquisition). Add these two *bonus* articulator isolations to your practice from Module Two to achieve some expert-level phthong isolation!

Exercise 5A: Tongue Arching in Motion—Moving the Mountain

Recall the tongue arching you did in Module Two. To begin, you tucked your tongue tip behind your bottom teeth and arched the body of your tongue toward your alveolar ridge. Try that now on a flow of noisy breath or voice. Try to arch the tongue body as far forward as it can physically go, and as high toward the roof of the mouth as it can go without obstructing the flow. If you obstruct by accident, congratulations! You've just found the line between shaping and obstructing. Play around on that line until you feel confident you're as high and as front as you can go while still remaining in phthong territory. Your tongue is in this amazing arch, not unlike a mountain or the crest of a wave.

> We're using two different images here for the action of arching the tongue: one of your tongue as a *mountain*, and one of your tongue as the *crest of a wave*. We're doing this on purpose! One image might make more sense to you than the other. Or one may serve you one day, but the next day you may find the other more useful. Or perhaps neither of them is useful to you. You're ultimately the expert on your own learning, so use what works best for you. Be flexible with yourself.

Try finding that same arched position of your mountain or wave crest, but this time as far back in your mouth as you can possibly go with your tongue tip still tucked behind your lower front teeth. Rather than arching the front of the tongue body, you will be arching the middle or the back of the tongue body. Again, if you need to play the line between shaping and obstructing to find that extreme high and extreme back tongue shape, go for it. Can you arch the tongue body that far back without retracting your tongue root? Perhaps not today. Many new skills require time, patience, and practice—put a pin in it, and you can test yourself on that skill later. The task now is to move the peak of that mountain from the front of the tongue body to the back of the tongue body, keeping the arch at the same

> *Tip*
>
> If moving the mountain is challenging for you right now, try whistling. Go from a high pitch to a low pitch. Even if you can't whistle (like one of the authors of this text), the *intention* of whistling from a high pitch to a low pitch will still do the trick. Seriously, try it. Do you feel your tongue changing shape as you do? Does it feel like moving the mountain or the crest of the wave from the front to the back?

high position toward the roof of your mouth. Try this first in silence, then with a voiced flow. Notice the sounds that result as this arched tongue moves back and forth in the mouth. Notice also if there are parts of your tongue that are more challenging to arch than others. Useful information to remember!

Exercise 5B: Tongue Cupping in Motion—Rolling the Blueberry

Now do the opposite of arching—cupping! As you did in Module Two, press down with the underside of your tongue, just behind your lower front teeth, to create a little cup, as if to hold a blueberry or small gumball. Actual blueberries or gumballs are recommended, but be mindful of any potential choking hazards! Now your task is to move the cup of your tongue (and thus, the blueberry) back as far as it can go while still remaining in your mouth. Try this a few times back and forth, first without voice and then with voice. Reward your efforts with a treat—perhaps a delicious blueberry or gumball?

All those positions you discovered in moving the mountain and rolling the blueberry produced shapes, and the shaping of voiced flow produced phthongs to add to your inventory of possible sounds. They are challenging exercises that call for regular practice if your goal is mastery. But if you can move mountains, think of what else you could do!

Now it's time to share your sophisticated phthong-making and phthong-mirroring skills with the rest of the class.

Exercise 6A: Phthonging in Community—Sharing the Monophthong With the Group

Arrange yourselves in a circle. One person begins by entering into a maraphthong for about 10 seconds, eventually holding on a shape and sound. That person will maintain that shape and sound, breathing both in and out through the shape, and then share that new shape/sound with the person next to them. When that person successfully mimics the sound and shape, then that person enters into their own maraphthong and repeats the process until all actors have both received and shared a monophthong.

Note that your keen "listening" skills, both aural and visual, are taking a leap forward into practicing in public. Sounds a little like the acting task, no?

Exercise 6B: Phthonging in Community—Combophthong Telephone

Circle up. One person begins by whispering a combination phthong, or "combophthong" (could be a diphthong but no more than a triphthong—yep, three shaped sounds!) into the ear of the person beside them. Note: it is *very* important that the person who begins the experiment remembers their original sound. Continue to pass the combination phthong quietly to each person in the circle until everyone has received it. The final person to receive it speaks the combination phthong out loud followed by the first person speaking their original combination phthong out loud. See how close, as a community, you got to recreating the sound exactly! Try this exercise again, but this time with the goal of precision as a community. How laser-focused and precise can you be as a class?

Up to this point, our phthonging exploration has left out one crucial layer: meaning. You've been doing what we might call "clinical" phthonging (or phthonging for the most variety) and investigating as you phthong: doing and noticing. Now, let's add meaning and see what shifts.

Exercise 6C: Phthonging in Community—Adding Meaning

You're at a meet and greet, so mingle! Using only phthongs to communicate, introduce yourself to people. Once you've done your introductions, you can have a conversation about how live theatre can contribute to society in the next 20 years. Phthong your hopes, goals, and dreams for this art form.

How did that go? Were you able to have complex, specific, and meaningful exchanges using just phthongs?

Sort of?

Are phthongs alone enough to create language? Not most of the time! Language seems to need more than shaping the flow to carry the complexity of human thought. You are going to have to obstruct the flow as well as shape it.

End of Module Wrap

As we come to the end of our phthonging for the time being, notice how much you allowed yourself to forget what you knew about "vowels" and how much you allowed yourself to explore new expressive territory called "phthongs" (or "phthonging" for the verb form). To review, we are defining "phthongs" as a shaping of the voiced flow using the following articulators:

Phthong Articulators

- Lips (orbicularis oris, risorius)
- Tongue Body (front, middle and back . . . but no tip and blade!)
- Velum (bonus)

Homework for this module:

> Keep phthonging! Practice "Moving the Mountain" and "Rolling the Blueberry" in your car, on the train, in the shower, on a walk—you get the picture: a lot!! Then practice your "clinical" phthonging, incorporating the nuanced shapes you practice in your mountain/blueberry rehearsals. Notice how many unfamiliar sounds you discover.

Table 3.1 Terms for Your Module Three Knowledge Celebration

KTS TERMS OF ART
- Descriptive knowledge
- Embodied knowledge
- Phthong
- Monophthong
- Maraphthong
- Shaping the Flow
- Obstructing the Flow
- Moving the Mountain
- Rolling the Blueberry

MODULE FOUR
EXPERIENCING OBSTRUCTED FLOW

In the last module we defined obstruction as "bringing vocal tract surfaces into closer or full contact with each other." Consider this question: closer than what? Well, phthongs of course! If you recall your phthong practice from the last module, there were moments you played with or crossed the line between shaping and obstructing. And there may have been moments when phthonging with meaning that you snuck in some obstruction here and there to assist in communicating your thought. That's because every spoken language contains obstruction as well as shaping.

Exercise 1A: Freeform Obstruction

You already know how to obstruct the flow, so do it. Experiment with *all the ways* you can obstruct the flow.

Wasn't I just making consonants?

Perhaps, but in the same way "vowel" is a limiting idea to our expressive territory, so is "consonant." You may be unconsciously beholden to the familiar sounds in your native language(s), or beholden to sounds you think *might* be in all languages. In order to open up into the unfamiliar, we're going to rename this speech action you may have previously called a consonant: **obstruent**. Pretty descriptive term, no? We're also going to go more extreme in our exploration of obstruents. In the previous skill-building exploration, if you fell into a habit of the familiar, or even if you fell into a habit of politeness, let that go!

Exercise 1B: Freeform Obstruction—Extreme Edition

Okay, really now—experiment with *all the ways* you can obstruct the flow. And don't limit your exploration to the plain old boring articulators you expect. Branch out! Perhaps you bring your hand to your mouth to obstruct, build up pressure from the lungs, and then explode some otherwise rude sound. Or perhaps you return to your ingressive speech sounds and find ways of obstructing *going in*. Or perhaps you revisit your most extreme gurns to see if there are new or exciting, messy or disgusting obstruents to explore through those shapes. *All the ways, all the ways, all the ways. Go!*

Do you feel as though your head may explode if you continue your extreme obstruction? Perhaps you experienced that this sheer number of obstruents could make continuous (connected) speech very difficult. Obstruction works best in the context of flow, so . . . we're gonna need some phthongs! But not yet. First, let's investigate more specifically what makes up an obstruent.

In the same way we broke down the component parts of a phthong in the last module (to review: something happens with your tongue *body*, something happens with your lips, and something *may* happen with your velum), let's do the same for obstruents.

Three-Ingredient Recipe for an Obstruent

Ingredient One: Flow

There has to be flow, and that flow can be either voiced (as in full phonation) or unvoiced (breath). And, at this point in our investigation, that flow can be egressive (going out) or ingressive (coming in).

How can you tell if an obstruent is voiced or unvoiced?

Try this: place your hand on your larynx and make an obstruent that is also a great imitation of a snake hissing. The lack of vibration under your hand at your larynx should reveal that no oscillation is happening at the vocal folds—meaning your glottis (the space between your vocal folds) is open. That's an *unvoiced* flow.

Now, keeping your hand on your larynx, make the sound of a bumble bee buzzing around the room. Your hand on your larynx should reveal that there *is* vibration happening at the vocal folds—meaning your glottis is closing and opening with the regular intervals of phonation. That's a voiced flow! Phonation, or voicing, is a type of obstruction that can happen simultaneously with other types of obstruction. If you return to your bee imitation, you can feel the vibration at your larynx and also perceive that there's a second place of obstruction along the path of the flow.

Try your bee sound again and switch the voicing on and off (bee/snake, bee/snake).

Exercise 2A: Obstruents—Varying the Voicing

Make an unvoiced obstruent. Test it with the hand-on-larynx test to be certain. Then send voice through your current obstructed shape to make the "voiced version" of your current obstruent. This task is similar to the one you just explored by going back and forth between the bee and snake sounds. Now try the opposite: make a different voiced obstruent and see if you can make the unvoiced version of that same obstruent.

Exactly what do you mean by "version"?
Great question. What do you think we mean?

Ingredient Two: Location
Ingredient two is all about obstruent location, location, location—and it's a big neighborhood! Think about all the possible locations where the flow can be obstructed to produce sound in the vocal tract—from lips to palate to **uvula** (the term for the "little grape" hanging down from the roof of your mouth, behind your velum) to all the way down in the larynx itself, and the spaces in between. All that is fair game for consonant real estate—a *much larger* area than the phthong neighborhood.

Exercise 2B: Obstruents—Varying the Location

Make some obstruents at all the locations in the vocal tract you can, from lips to larynx! While you explore, observe which locations feel less

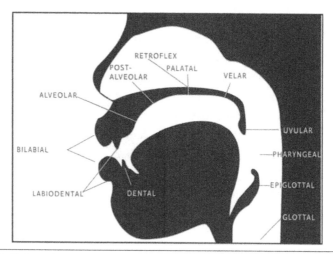

Figure 4.1 Obstruent Locations

familiar and which locations feel more familiar. Notice your response to both the unfamiliar and the familiar. Remember to breathe!

Ingredient Three: Action

You may have already started to notice that there are different degrees to which you can obstruct the flow of breath or voice. You can obstruct the flow a lot, a little, or somewhere in between. We'll get more specific about these different actions in the next module, but for now, know that you can make complete closures, partial closures, and closures that are so partial they may even remind you of a phthong.

Exercise 2C: Obstruents—Varying the Action

Try obstructing the flow *a lot*. Make a complete closure somewhere in the vocal tract, build up pressure, and then explode it. Do this a few times, in a few different locations, some with voice and some without.

Next, try obstructing the flow ever so slightly. Gently purse your two lips toward each other without touching—and then let them glide apart. Try that on a flow of voice. You're obstructing the flow to such a small degree that if you used an unvoiced flow, there may not be any sound at all.

Finally, revisit your snake and bee sounds. Do those sounds feel like obstructing the flow somewhere in the middle of our obstruent intensity spectrum? Try to find more obstruents like that.

Exercise 3A: Advanced Obstruction—"I Will Now Perform . . ."

Now that you have this simple recipe at the ready (flow, location, and action), play around with all three ingredients as you find, yet again, all the ways you can obstruct the flow. Focus on *feeling* each obstruction at the specific point inside your vocal tract where you're making it. Get curious about how you might describe that feeling. Does it feel like a buzz? Two surfaces moving dynamically apart like an explosion? Be creative! Then speak your description out loud: "This is a tongue to the teeth buzz with voice," or "This is a no-phonation uvulatory explosion!" After some practice with this, find a partner and take turns stating the type of obstruent you will perform, describing each of the three ingredients in whatever imaginative way makes sense to you. For example: "I will now perform a throaty cough with voicing." Then do it!

Add Some Phthongs to Those Obstruents

When exploring an obstruent, it's useful to add phthongs at various places around the obstruent to hear its full acoustic effect. Test this out. When performing an obstruent, do it first on its own. Then, add a phthong (*any* phthong) after the obstruent. Then add a phthong before the obstruent. Then add a phthong before *and* after the obstruent. Here's the pattern: O; O+P; P+O; P+O+P. We encourage you to use this technique now and forever!

Exercise 3B: Advanced Obstruction With Phthongs

You've earned them . . . Now add phthongs to your exploration, moving from obstruent to phthong, however the mood strikes you. Start slowly at first, then pick up the pace.

Listen to that! On your path toward language, you have traveled from silence, to noisy breath, to creak, to full phonation, to shaping the flow, to obstructing the flow in a vast variety of ways, to combining both shaping and obstructing so that now you've arrived at language!

You may not recognize this as language yet because you're still in "clinical" mode. In order to move our experimentation from the clinical into the expressive, we'll need to string our speech gestures into a connected flow, and to use that flow of sounds to communicate with the people around us. This will give our sounds meaning and transform sound play into language. We have a name for this language that you now find yourself instantly capable of speaking. It is called **Outlandish**, and as you can no doubt guess, it is the language spoken by the people of the lost continent of Outlandis. And now, by you.

Exercise 4A: Outlandish Debate

Debate is a huge part of Outlandish culture. Get a debate partner. In Outlandish, one of you will argue to keep cheese production a thriving industry in the continent of Outlandis and argue to get rid of chocolate production *forever*. The other will argue to keep Outlandis's chocolate production and thus cut cheese production *forever*.

If you're a skilled group of debaters, other important, *essential*, topics might include keeping cats or keeping dogs, keeping red or keeping blue, keeping social media or keeping television.

Exercise 4B: Outlandish Love Poems

Outlandians are not just debaters. They are lovers as well. Switch partners. This time, instead of debating, create an extemporaneous praise poem for your partner in Outlandish. Express all the wonderful things you either know or imagine about them.

Exercise 4C: Outlandish Tech Support

One person, desperate, calls Outlandish tech support for their phone, laptop, or tablet issue. The other person is the tech support customer service representative. Let the conflict begin.

Exercise 4D: Outlandish Singing

Because Outlandish is, well, outlandish, it can be easy to forget good vocal practice. The great Outlandish singing traditions will help with that. In a circle:

- The Outlandian Pop Star will sing their biggest hit.
- The Outlandian Broadway Star will sing their 11 o'clock number.

- The Outlandian M.C. will bust a mean Outlandish rhyme.
- The Outlandian Opera Star will bring the house down with their concert hall-filling vocal skills.

Exercise 4E: Outlandish Jazz Band

Form groups of two to four people. Each group, one at a time, will lay down an Outlandish obstruent or obstruent/phthong combination track to a jazz song. Once each group has entered the song and established the rhythm and melody, one solo vocalist will use Outlandish to riff and scat and create jazz magic. Once their solo is complete, the band continues with the melody while another soloist takes a turn. You can stop when you've reached maximum Outlandish coolness, but not before.

Need more Outlandish exercise ideas? Visit your web resources for hours of Outlandish play. Go now. Hurry.

 Web Resource 6: Outlandish Exercises

End of Module Wrap

The homework for this module is simple:

> Revisit your "Clinical Outlandish"—no meaning or communication, but rather exploring maximum obstruent and phthong variety. With care to use good vocal practice, spend some time with unfamiliar locations in particular. This will serve you well in the next module.

Table 4.1 Terms for Your Module Four Knowledge Celebration:

KTS TERMS OF ART	ROOF OF MOUTH
• Obstruent	• Uvula
• Outlandish	
• Obstruent Recipe (flow, location, action)	

PART TWO
THE POSSIBILITIES IN LANGUAGE

MODULE FIVE

EXPERIENCING OBSTRUENTS IN LANGUAGE

We have journeyed from silence to making *every vocal tract sound possible*. Now it's time to strategically limit our exploration. While Outlandish did us the great service of opening up possibility, we need to begin narrowing our focus for two reasons:

- Every sound is certainly interesting, but every sound does not occur in language.
- As of this printing, there are no plays or films written in the language of Outlandish.

As such, we've now arrived at the moment when we need to define more specifically the obstruents that occur in existing languages on this planet. Our three-ingredient recipe still applies, but there are some sounds we can rule out.

Reflection

What outrageous vocal tract sounds do you hypothesize will not occur in language?

Some possible answers could be:

- Too many obstruents in a row may make your head explode. Obstruent clusters in language will be limited to about five or so before a phthong will be required, with some notable exceptions.
- Ingressive phthongs occur in very few languages, and even within those languages they are used infrequently.
- Sounds that are too difficult* or inefficient for *any* human to make in connected speech won't be found in (any actual) language.

Warning

"Too difficult" is a relative phrase! A sound too difficult for you might be quite easy for someone who speaks a language in which that sound occurs. When we say, "too difficult for any human," we mean speech actions more like bringing your bottom lip to touch your velum, or bringing your tongue tip to your uvula. If you're trying to determine whether or not a sound is too difficult or inefficient to occur in any language, before passing judgment, ponder whether there *might* be a group of speakers who could make that sound with efficiency.

Getting Specific With Obstruent Ingredients, Part 1: Actions

Web Resource 7: Obstruent Actions and the River

In the last module we broadly explored action (our third of three obstruent "ingredients") by obstructing the flow a lot, a little, or somewhere in between. Let's get more granular with that spectrum. We'll also limit our exploration to *egressive* flow which travels from the lungs up and out of the body. We will use the movement of a river as a metaphorical touchstone. *Most* rivers flow in one direction, as do most languages. (There are notable exceptions, of course, but we will stick with one singular direction for now.)

Let's begin with the most obstructed actions that lead to speech sounds, and then move toward the least obstructed.

Stop Plosives: Imagine a dam in a river. The dam comes down and *stops* the water from flowing. Water pressure builds up behind the dam, and then when the dam is lifted, the flow *explodes* forward. A stop plosive (also called a stop or a plosive) has the same steps. There is a stop with full contact between two articulators or between one articulator (the movable part) and a **point of articulation** (a stationary part). Examples include but are not limited to two lips together, or tongue tip to alveolar ridge. Air pressure builds up behind that stop. Then, when the pressure breaks open the closure, a sound occurs. Try some.

In order for pressure to build up in the stop plosives you just tried, there was another closure that happened. Can you guess what it is?

Nasals: Have you ever heard of a sluice? It's a human-made device to fork the direction of a river. Instead of flowing on the main path, it flows on a modified path. So does the nasal obstruent! Instead of flowing out of the mouth, a nasal obstruent closes off the oral cavity (another way to describe the mouth) at a "front door" location and keeps the "back door" port between the throat and nose open. The flow is then redirected to come out only through the nose. You already know the term for the movable part of the roof of your mouth: velum. It is the upper surface of the oral cavity and also the lower surface of the nasal cavity. The term for the back wall of the throat is the **pharynx.** This port that "sluices" the flow through the nasal cavity has a name that combines these two terms: the **velopharyngeal port**.

In order to create the buildup of pressure required for a stop plosive, the velopharyngeal port must be closed by raising the velum. For a nasal, the velopharyngeal port must be open by lowering the velum. If you speak a language that has nasals, you're likely accomplishing this lowering of the velum without needing to think about it. For our work, it's useful for you to put some consciousness into this action. Try making a nasal. Then temporarily block the flow at the velopharyngeal port by raising your velum. Then make the nasal again with your velum lowered, allowing the flow to resume through the nose. That lowering, raising, and lowering of the velum may result in a feeling similar to when you blow your nose.

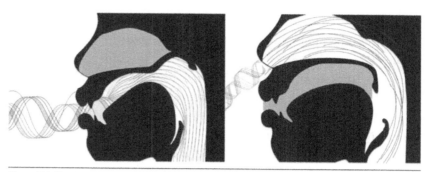

Figure 5.1 The Velopharyngeal Port: Closed and Open

Trills: Like a riverboat with revolving paddles that continuously make contact with water, a trill is a sequence of repeated, periodic contact between an articulator and a point of articulation. It sounds a lot like the action of a stop plosive, so let's discover how it's different. Start by repeating a "b" sound a few times. What you're doing here is creating a series of stop plosives. Now, try fluttering your lips on voice, as if you were doing an impression of a motorboat. Go back and forth between "b-b-b-b" and the flutter action. You may notice that the stop plosive is a muscular action: lips come together by virtue of muscular force, and when that contact is broken, you get a "b" sound. Conversely, when you flutter your lips, they come together repeatedly by virtue of a different type of force. That force comes from increasing the flow from your lungs, and then your lips go on a ride. Hence, riverboat paddles!

Sidebar on Trills

Does the fluttering action of a trill remind you of anything we've already covered? Check the end of this module to test your theory.

Taps/Flaps: Taps and flaps are only one revolution of the riverboat paddle—one instance of contact before the articulators go to other jobs. For taps, the articulator starts at its home base, moves to the point of articulation to make momentary contact, and then returns to its home base. For example, when tapping your tongue to your alveolar ridge, your tongue tip starts wherever it comfortably rests, curls up to hit the alveolar ridge, and then returns back to where it started. For flaps, the articulator starts in one location, moves to the point of articulation to make momentary contact, and then travels to a place different from its starting location. For a *flap* at the alveolar ridge, the tongue tip starts *behind* the alveolar ridge, hits the alveolar ridge, and makes its way to a resting place in front of the alveolar ridge. Try some taps and flaps at various locations in the vocal tract.

Fricatives: In our river analogy, imagine white water rapids. There may be lots of small and large rocks in the river, but the flow of water still moves swiftly around them, creating a sort of friction sound. This is precisely how a fricative is made in the vocal tract! Articulators and points of articulation come close to each other, not touching, and the resultant sound is the breath or voiced flow trying to get past the closeness of the articulators. Make some fricative sounds. Begin by imitating rushing water, or a particularly fierce, lashing wind. You may notice that there is *some contact* between surfaces even though we're defining fricatives as the articulators and points of articulation coming *close* to one another. When we're describing a fricative, we want to be sure to define the location by the **point of obstruent focus**. If you make a sound that means "lower your voice"—"shhhhh"—the sides of your tongue may indeed touch the roof of your mouth or your upper molars, but the point of obstruent focus is where the sound is being made. Where do you feel the actual friction? Perhaps you feel it in an area behind the alveolar ridge, yet there is no contact there.

Approximants: If fricatives are like lots of rocks in the river making white water friction, then an approximant is like one small stone in the river. The stone is certainly obstructing the flow, but only to the smallest degree. Think back to when we were exploring obstructing the flow "a little bit" in the last module. Those obstruents were approximants. For approximants, there's no actual contact between articulator and point of articulation, but they are certainly quite close to each other! And if you hang out on the sound of an approximant long enough, you might find you've moved into phthong territory. Take some time to explore the boundary between phthong and obstruent—where do you think one begins and the other ends?

Laterals: If a huge boulder obstructed the middle of the river, the flow of water would go around the sides. This is precisely what happens when we make a lateral, and the boulder is your tongue! To make a lateral obstruent, seal off somewhere down the midline of your mouth with your tongue, and keep the sides of the mouth clear for flow. For example, curl your tongue tip up to your alveolar ridge. Then bunch the side edges of your tongue in (remember hot dog tongue?), so there's an open channel for flow along the sides of the mouth. Send a flow of breath through that shape. Then send a flow of voice through that shape. Is the sound flowing out the sides of the mouth (and *not* down the center line)? If so, you're making a lateral!

Side Note

Until we got to laterals, we assumed that all previous actions we'd defined were central sounds, meaning the flow travels down the midline of the oral cavity. We will continue to uncover hidden assumptions as we go!

Affricates: Speaking of hidden assumptions, we have been assuming that all obstruents in language are made by one singular action—or articulation—in the vocal tract. An affricate is a combination of two actions, or a **double articulation**: a stop plosive and a fricative. Imagine that a dam has been dropped on our river to stop the flow completely, and then that dam springs a few leaks, allowing some flow to release through those small openings. An affricate begins with a stop, and, when the flow breaks open that closure, the articulator stays close to the point of articulation to create some friction in the release.

You may also have assumed that all obstruents in language have an **airstream mechanism** that is **pulmonic**: a one-way flow of air from the lungs through the vocal tract and out into the world. In fact, we chose to focus on egressive sounds at the beginning of this module, and that choice may have contributed to this assumption. There are some obstruents in language that are *not* pulmonic, meaning they don't use flow that comes from the lungs. Instead, the flow initiates inside the vocal tract.

How is that possible??

Just wait; you'll see. These obstruents are aptly called **non-pulmonics**. Let's dive into them to discover what the airstream mechanism is for each.

Clicks: What does the word "click" mean to you? Do some clicks now. How are you making that sound?

Quite a few things are happening as you click. You're closing off the oral cavity at a certain location, possibly at your two lips or at your alveolar ridge with your tongue tip/blade, and you're starting to suck in. When you release the closure, a sound occurs.

But what's causing the sound?

An airstream mechanism known as **velaric suction**. When you make a click, you're creating a vacuum between a front point of closure and a back point of closure at your velum. Without that "backdoor" contact between the velum and the middle of the tongue body, you wouldn't be able to create a click.

If clicks are velaric suction, what is the airstream mechanism for all the pulmonic obstruents we've already explored?

Great question. It's not suction, because the air is flowing out. Since the origin for the airstream is the lungs and the flow is egressive, this airstream mechanism is defined as **pulmonic pressure**.

So, if pressure is egressive, does that mean suction is ingressive?

You got it. But not all suction is velaric. And not all pressure is pulmonic.

Ejectives: This non-pulmonic obstruent's airstream mechanism is **glottalic pressure**. Before we unpack that for you, try to make one with this description to guide you: an ejective is like making a stop plosive while holding your breath.

If the pressure is glottalic, that means the flow starts at the glottis, and the air trapped between the glottis and the closure in the mouth is the air you're able to use for the ejective. If you're unfamiliar with ejectives in language, you may recognize these sounds from beatboxing!

Voiced Implosives: **Glottalic suction** is the airstream mechanism for voiced implosives. As you know, suction denotes the flow will be ingressive—just like in a click. Also, like clicks, there is a complete closure, or stop, at some point in the oral cavity, and the velum is raised to prevent any airflow from escaping through the nasal cavity. Do that. At the same time, hold your breath. Create some suction to bring your larynx down over the column of air trapped between the oral closure and the glottis. Release the closure in the oral cavity, at the same time sucking air in to create an implosion. By moving your vocal folds over the air, they vibrate, giving you the *voiced* portion of the voiced implosive. (When voicing in this way, you're moving the folds over the air, as opposed to moving the air through the folds, which is what you do in voiced pulmonic sounds. Cool, right?) Try some of these sounds on your own, and then refer to the sound files for examples.

     Web Resource 8: Non-Pulmonics Audio

Getting Specific With Obstruent Ingredients, Part 2: Locations

Identifying the locations of obstruent focus can be pretty intuitive, and in our explorations thus far you have made obstruents in all the places in the list that follows. But it's valuable to get specific about the locations, both descriptively and kinesthetically, so that you may *choose* to make a sound at a particular location if directed, or so that you may *identify* a sound happening at a particular location. These are super useful skills for the complex task of accent acquisition.

Let's begin from the top of the vocal tract and travel all the way to the bottom:

- Bilabial: bringing both lips together or toward one another
- Labiodental: bringing lower lip to, toward, or behind upper teeth
- Dental/alveolar/postalveolar: bringing tongue tip (or blade) to the upper teeth, to the alveolar ridge, or to the back slope of the alveolar ridge
- Retroflex: curling tongue tip back to or toward the palate

- Palatal: bringing front of the tongue body to or toward the palate
- Velar: bringing middle of the tongue body to or toward the velum
- Uvular: bringing back of the tongue body to or toward the uvula
- Pharyngeal: bringing the tongue root straight back to or toward the pharynx
- Epiglottal: bringing the flap of tissue at the top of the windpipe to or towards the windpipe.

Web Resource 9: Sounds at the Epiglottis

- Glottal: bringing the vocal folds themselves to or toward one another

Why do some of these location names give me more information than others?

Web Resource 10: KTS Tongue Dance

We have just the thing to help! We lovingly refer to this as **The KTS Tongue Dance**. It must be seen *and* experienced. So, at your earliest convenience, visit your web resources to learn, love, and live the tongue dance!

Exercise 1: Obstruent Mapping

Now that you've mastered the tongue dance and can also differentiate the actions of obstruents, it's time for a full class exercise to map out the terrain.

Half the class will be the vocal tract, depicting a person facing the left. You will need to cast the following roles:

- Two people as the lips
- One person as the velum
- One or two people as the tongue (tip/blade and body/root if you have two people)
- One or two people as the vocal folds (and thereby, the glottis as well)

Those are the moving parts . . . other than the air! As you know, these are the articulators.

For the non-moving parts—or the points of articulation—you may have people cast in the roles of teeth, alveolar ridge, palate, uvula, and the back wall of the pharynx (depending on the size of your group), or you may create physical landmarks from whatever objects are on hand to signify these locations. Casting a person or prop as the nose and lungs would also be useful!

All the rest of the people are the flow—either voiced or unvoiced, depending on the instruction. The group will make a selection for each part of our three-part obstruent recipe: flow (voiced or unvoiced), a location, and an obstruent action. The flow will then come from the lungs and move through the vocal tract, making the sound at the point of obstruent focus before leaving through the lips or nose.

Work through several pulmonic obstruent actions, several locations, and both voiced and unvoiced sounds. We suggest you trade roles at some point so everyone can have a chance at being the flow.

Web Resource 11: Obstruent Mapping

A video of this exercise is housed in your web resources. You can follow that model, or you can make your own!

End of Module Wrap

Homework to solidify the work from this module is to practice your KTS Tongue Dance! Get great at it. Do it from memory. It's silly, but also incredibly valuable embodied knowledge for where we're headed next.

**Sidebar on Trills

If you likened the action of a trill to the action of phonation itself, you were correct! Flow causing the vocal folds to come together and apart to create voice is exactly the same type of effect that's happening when you make a trill! It's called the Bernoulli Effect, and it's also the phenomenon that keeps airplanes in the air. If you're so inclined to "speech geek-out" on the science of sound, feel free to deepen your exploration to your heart's content.

Table 5.1 Terms for your Module Five Knowledge Celebration

AIRSTREAM MECHANISMS

- Pulmonic
- Non-pulmonic
- Glottalic pressure
- Glottalic suction
- Pulmonic pressure
- Velaric suction

LOCATIONS

- Bilabial
- Labiodental
- Dental
- Alveolar
- Postalveolar
- Retroflex
- Palatal
- Velar
- Uvular
- Epiglottal
- Glottal
- Point of obstruent focus
- Point of articulation

ACTIONS (also referred to as MANNERS OF ARTICULATION

- Stop plosive
- Nasal
- Trill
- Tap
- Flap
- Fricative
- Approximant
- Lateral
- Affricate
- Click
- Voiced implosive
- Ejective
- Double articulation

ANATOMY

- Pharynx
- Velopharyngeal port
- Epiglottis

KTS TERM OF ART

- The KTS Tongue Dance

MODULE SIX
EXPERIENCING THE EMPTY CHARTS—CONSONANTS

On our journey toward language, we've explored an extraordinary number of obstruents—nearly all of them! We've explored vast swaths of vocal tract territories and likely discovered new and exciting locations. As such, it would be useful for us to have a way of organizing all of these obstruents, just as we might chart new geographic discoveries on a map. Fortunately, the **International Phonetic Association** (IPA) has done just that. They have created an **International Phonetic Alphabet** (also the IPA—confusing, we know) as a means of describing any speech action observed in the world, regardless of language, all within a handy chart! This is incredibly useful, but it is also imperfect. We will find, as we explore this handy organizational tool, that there are flaws in the system. The way the information is organized reveals some cultural biases of the IPA (the organization), as well as some hidden assumptions and limitations of the IPA (the tool). But, as we have noted in the principles (and precepts) of this work, biases are inevitable. We make ourselves aware of biases so we can distinguish them from absolute truths.

You will notice that the non-pulmonics have their own smaller chart below the larger pulmonic chart. One might infer that that smaller chart, lower on the page, is a sub-chart of sounds or is less important than the

CONSONANTS (PULMONIC)

	Bilabial	Labiodental	Dental	Alveolar	Post-Alveolar	Retroflex	Palatal	Velar	Uvular	Pharyngeal	Glottal
Plosive											
Nasal											
Trill											
Tap or Flap											
Fricative											
Lateral fricative											
Approximant											
Lateral approximant											

Where symbols appear in pairs, the one to the right represents a voiced consonant. Shaded areas denote articulations judged impossible.

CONSONANTS (NON-PULMONIC)

Clicks	Voiced Implosives	Ejectives
Bilabial	Bilabial	Examples:
Dental	Dental/alveolar	Bilabial
(Post)alveolar	Palatal	Dental/alveolar
Palatoalveolar	Velar	Velar
Alveolar lateral	Uvular	Alveolar fricative

Figure 6.1 The Empty Consonant Charts

pulmonic consonant chart. This is not so! The IPA wanted to get the chart condensed enough to be printed on one page of a book without shrinking the type beyond the limits of legibility. Hence, they separated non-pulmonics from pulmonics into two tables. As a way of potentially upending a bias, let's start with non-pulmonics.

Remember, no sound is either better or worse, more important or less important, than another. And, as performers, it's useful to have the skills to create any sound in any accent or language. Let's go, mouth-letes!

Note that now that we're getting into the nitty-gritty of all the obstruent actions in human language (really—all of them), you are hereby permissioned to use the *newly expansive* term "consonant" to describe each of these actions.

Web Resource 12: Printable Non-Pulmonic Placards

Printable placards in your web resources have non-pulmonic actions and locations, as seen in the chart in Figure 6.2.

Notice the organization of the column and row headers on this chart. Place the placards on the ground, organized in the same way.

Before we try making these consonants, let's interrogate how the chart in Figure 6.2 has organized our ingredients. Some things to notice:

In the non-pulmonic chart, we see a limited number of locations listed—only the locations where that action has been observed in some language. Really, this isn't so much a chart as it is a list.

Second, we're coming across the term **palatoalveolar** for the first time. This doesn't mean that you bring your palate to the alveolar ridge. That would be pretty impressive if you could figure that one out! Instead, the term refers to a type of **coarticulation**, meaning there are two simultaneous points of obstruent focus—one at the palate and one at the alveolar ridge. Palatoalveolar is a specialized description that shows up only in this non-pulmonic chart. See if you can figure it out! More coarticulations to come.

Finally, notice that under the ejectives column you first see the word "Examples," followed by a colon. This means that, when it comes to ejectives, these are some possible placements, but they are not finite or fixed. When we get to ejectives, in addition to trying the examples provided, try out some that aren't listed as well.

CONSONANTS (NON-PULMONIC)

Clicks	Voiced Implosives	Ejectives
Bilabial	Bilabial	Examples:
Dental	Dental/alveolar	Bilabial
(Post)alveolar	Palatal	Dental/alveolar
Palatoalveolar	Velar	Velar
Alveolar lateral	Uvular	Alveolar fricative

Figure 6.2 Non-Pulmonic Empty Chart

Exercise 1: The Empty Chart, Non-Pulmonics

Once the non-pulmonic placards are organized on the floor, step inside each "cell" and try the action at that location. Move down the Clicks column. Using the definitions of locations and actions you have at your disposal, see if you can make each click. In a series of images starting with Figure 6.3, Dot, our model student, demonstrates how you might explore *your* floor charts. (Yes! There are more charts to come!)

Then move onto the Voiced Implosives column, followed by the Ejectives column.

Note: You may need a reminder of how we define each action, and that's perfectly fine. There were a lot of terms to know in Module Five, so it may take some time and practice before you feel as though you own that embodied knowledge.

I'm curious why we're not learning the symbols now as well.

One step at a time. Because the symbols represent speech actions, we feel it's more important to first define an action and then perform it before we take the leap to using a symbol to represent it. Symbols will come, and they will be useful as a shorthand—placeholders standing in for the full description of a speech action. But they are not the focus of what we are doing in this text. The *doing* is.

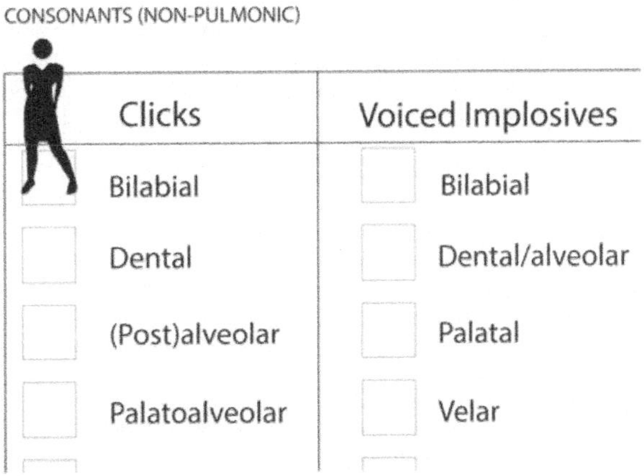

CONSONANTS (NON-PULMONIC)

	Clicks		Voiced Implosives
	Bilabial		Bilabial
	Dental		Dental/alveolar
	(Post)alveolar		Palatal
	Palatoalveolar		Velar

Figure 6.3 Dot Exploring the Clicks Column

It's time to begin an exploration of the Pulmonic Consonant Chart. Let's take a look at an empty version (Figure 6.4), without symbols but including descriptive text that will help us define these articulatory gestures.

Notice all the locations in the top row. If you've been practicing the KTS Tongue Dance, there will be no new information here. Perhaps it might be wise to practice that dance again now. Take your time; we'll wait.

You may notice that there's something unique about the Dental/Alveolar/Postalveolar column. Notice the lack of column division in all but the Fricative row. Do you have some theories as to why the IPA might organize the chart in this way? We will come back to this. In the meantime, stay curious about the answer.

You also may notice that the locations are organized from the front of the vocal tract (bilabial) to the back (glottal). If you were to see a whole person attached to these points of articulation, they would be facing to the left, and the person's vocal tract would take a sharp right turn down to the lungs as we moved from the uvular to the pharyngeal locations, the same as in the Obstruent Mapping exercise in the last module.

Have you noticed that affricates don't appear in the action column? This chart will only identify singular articulations. Double articulations will show up somewhere else.

CONSONANTS (PULMONIC)

	Bilabial	Labiodental	Dental	Alveolar	Postalveolar	Retroflex	Palatal	Velar	Uvular	Pharyngeal	Glottal
Plosive											
Nasal											
Trill											
Tap or Flap											
Fricative											
Lateral fricative											
Approximant											
Lateral approximant											

Where symbols appear in pairs, the one to the right represents a voiced consonant. Shaded areas denote articulations judged impossible.

Figure 6.4 The Empty Pulmonic Chart

Notice the text at the bottom of the chart: "Symbols to the right in a cell are voiced, to the left are voiceless. Shaded areas denote articulations judged impossible." You may notice that our blank chart doesn't include any shaded areas. Part of this next project will be to identify any of these recipes that prove to be physically impossible. We have removed the shaded areas so your investigation can be based solely on your own experiments, and not on any preconceived ideas the chart provides.

What do you mean by "impossible"? For example, I can't really do a voiced implosive yet, so for today it's impossible for me. But I see other people doing them. So, are we testing what's impossible for any human?

Yes! That is precisely your project. You're testing what would be physically impossible for *any* human, not just the humans in your room, school, country, or continent.

Before we begin to play within this chart, it may be useful to see how it is actually a schematic representation (shown in Figure 6.5) of where these sounds get realized in your vocal tract. You know this, but seeing it graphically can help solidify the understanding.

Web Resource 13: Printable Pulmonic Placards

Exercise 2A: The Empty Chart, Pulmonics—
Individual Exploration

For this exercise you will need the printable placards in your web resources for the pulmonic consonant actions and locations. Place the placards on the ground for all column and row headers as laid out in the Empty Chart in Figure 6.4, in the same location as your person facing left from Obstruent Mapping in the last module. Take time to explore each "cell" and perform *both* possible consonants. When to the left of the cell, perform the unvoiced (or voiceless) version. When to the right of the cell, perform the voiced version. Check out how Dot is doing it (Figure 6.6)!

Try doing an entire row. For example, try the trills row. When you get to the huge cell of dental/alveolar/postalveolar, perform the action at all three points of articulation and notice the difference in sound, if any.

After you've completed an entire row, try an entire column. Can you perform all the actions at the bilabial location, for instance?

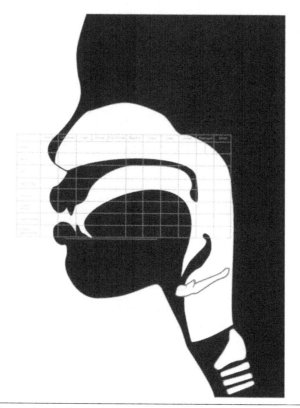

Figure 6.5 The Empty Pulmonic Chart in the Mouth

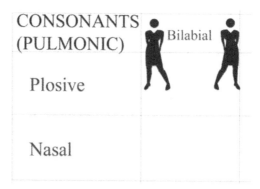

Figure 6.6 Dot Exploring Each Side of the Bilabial Plosive Cell

Reflection

Discuss as a group what you've discovered. Are there confusions about the location or action definitions? In a community effort, make sure you get clarity about the definitions. Were there any consonant recipes that were physically impossible?

Exercise 2B: The Empty Chart, Pulmonics—Group Exploration

Start with all the cells in the Fricative row. As a group, spend some time exploring both sides of each cell, meaning both the voiced and unvoiced versions of the same articulation. Do any of them seem physically impossible?

Exercise 3: Other Symbols—Group Exploration

As a group, spend some time exploring the "Other Symbols" section of the chart (Figure 6.7).

Use what you know about coarticulations and double articulations from your exploration of clicks and affricates and follow the recipes of the symbol names to experiment with the speech gestures you think the names are describing. Take your time and stay curious about testing the ingredients of each consonant. Make sure you're clear on the definitions of each, but don't get too hung up on "getting it right." The journey is much more important. In fact, one of the Other Symbols is defined on the chart as two simultaneous obstruent actions. You won't know what those actions are until we get the symbols! And that's okay.

End of Module Wrap

We will be using *all the possible sounds* in the next module. In preparation for that, your homework is to take a few recipes from the Empty Chart and see if you can perform the sound according to the recipe. Using the consonant descriptors in the following list, perform each consonant action as described. Remember, the three ingredients (voiced/unvoiced flow; location; action) are your guides. Just as you sounded out words when first learning to read, so too you must "sound out" and feel each ingredient in the consonant.

- Voiced bilabial stop-plosive
- Voiced velar stop-plosive
- Voiced bilabial implosive
- Voiced velar approximant
- Voiced velar nasal
- Unvoiced alveolar fricative
- Voiced labial-velar approximant
- Voiced bilabial approximant
- Unvoiced lateral palatal fricative
- Unvoiced bilabial ejective
- Unvoiced postalveolar click
- Voiced alveolar stop-plosive
- Voiced retroflex lateral approximant

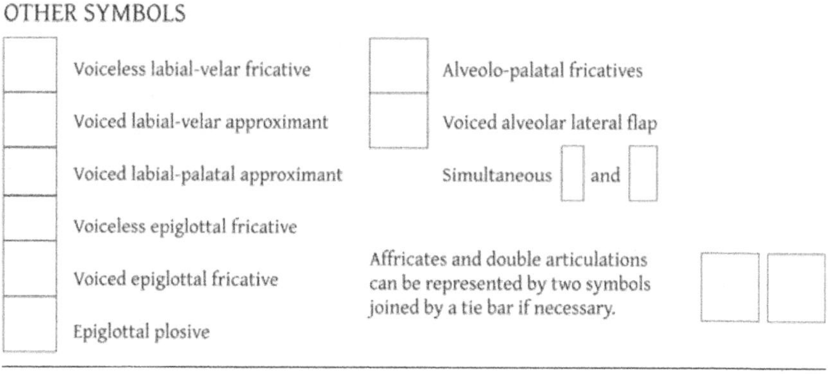

OTHER SYMBOLS

	Voiceless labial-velar fricative		Alveolo-palatal fricatives
	Voiced labial-velar approximant		Voiced alveolar lateral flap
	Voiced labial-palatal approximant	Simultaneous [ ] and [ ]	
	Voiceless epiglottal fricative		
	Voiced epiglottal fricative	Affricates and double articulations can be represented by two symbols joined by a tie bar if necessary.	
	Epiglottal plosive		

Figure 6.7 "Other Symbols" Empty Chart

Table 6.1 Terms for Your Module Six Knowledge Celebration

International Phonetic Association
International Phonetic Alphabet
Coarticulation

MODULE SEVEN
EXPERIENCING LANGUAGE

We asked you to forget what you know about language so we could discover the component parts together and open up our descriptive and embodied understanding of all the possibilities in language. You've done that with aplomb. Great. And at this point in our journey, it's also useful to acknowledge that language already exists in your vocal tract in the form of the languages you speak every day. There are muscular actions and coupled speech gestures that feel familiar to you because you use them a lot. You also have a starting position for your articulators, or "home base," that is not only familiar, but also the most ideal posture for making all the sounds in your language(s) in the precise way you choose to make them. Yes, your sounds are choices! Perhaps they are or have been largely unconscious choices. Moving forward, we will encourage you to bring more awareness to what is familiar. It is useful both to acknowledge the existence of this home base and these familiar speech gestures, and to disrupt that posture and those gestures in order to find new ones.

Recall the beginning of our journey when we were figuring out what is actually required for human language. We started with silence, then added noisy breath, creak, full phonation, and shaping the flow into phthongs. Then, by finally adding obstructing the flow *by any means*, we arrived at our first language: Outlandish. This is the widest our language scope will go because Outlandish includes any sound that is physically possible.

It's now time to narrow our focus to only sounds that do *or could* exist in language observed on this planet. You've just explored all the consonants that are physically possible in language by going through the Empty Consonant Charts in Module Six. And back in Module Three, you explored the infinite variety of phthong shapes. When we put the two components of phthongs and charted consonants together, we arrive at a language that has a more narrowed variety of sounds than Outlandish. But as you've discovered, looking more deeply into the articulatory actions used in human language has opened up a much more detailed landscape of possibilities than we likely experienced in Outlandish. Though we've limited our scope somewhat, the range of options available in this new exploratory language is still incredibly vast and specific.

All *possible* Consonants on the Chart + All Phthong Shapes = New Language!

An Articulator Warm-Up

Before we dive into our new language, it will be useful to identify some ingredients for a good warm-up:

GURN: Start with a slow-motion, unvoiced gurn. How slow can you go? Start to speed the gurn up. Then add some gentle phonation to your exhalations, allowing new breath in whenever you need it. Now, slow down the voiced gurn for a moment or two. Let it go. Lean forward and shake out your face.

STRETCH: Come back up from that and bring your hands to your sternum (also known as your breastbone). Pull down on your sternum and advance your jaw. Then stretch your chin up toward the ceiling. Do you feel a stretch across the front of your neck? To increase that stretch, trace a rainbow arc with your chin from side to side. Bring your chin back to center and down again.

MASSAGE: Bring your fingertips to your masseter muscle and give it a massage. Then, let that massage travel up to your temporalis muscle. Finally, do a few Expert Jaw Releases.

WAKE UP YOUR ARTICULATORS: Lightly pinch the skin above your upper lip—the upper part of your orbicularis oris. Give it a wiggle. Do the same for the skin below your lower lip, the lower part of your orbicularis oris. Lightly pinch your lip corners and give them a wiggle. Next, tuck your pinkies in your lip corners, and stretch them wide. Then stretch them up into a smile, then down into a frown. Stretch one lip corner up and the other down to form a diagonal. Then stretch them on the opposite diagonal. Release your lip corners and do an unvoiced bilabial trill.

Tuck your tongue tip behind your lower front teeth and arch your tongue body outside of your mouth. Let it release back into your mouth. Repeat a few times as slowly or quickly as you like. Then stick your tongue outside of your mouth. Bunch it skinny like a hot dog. Spread it wide like a pancake. Repeat a few times. Bring your tongue inside of your mouth and brace the side edges against the insides of your upper molars. Release. Repeat a few times.

Let your tongue relax for the moment and have a yawn. Once that yawn has run its course, do a Professional Yawn. Then two sideways yawns. Lastly, do a Master Yawn. Do you feel your velum stretching up and spreading wide?

Exercise 1: Easing Into a New Language

Start some gentle micro-movements, or **shimmers**, around the home base for your articulators. Then enter into an easy maraphthong by creating more distinctive shapes with your tongue, lips, and velum. Begin to add in consonant sounds. Are the first sounds that are added familiar to you? If so, begin to add in the less familiar. If the opposite is true for you, remember to also include the familiar. Check in with your kinesthetic experience: Do you experience certain parts of your vocal tract getting less attention than others? Have you visited your palate in a while? What about pharyngeal consonants? Something else? Make sure you're experiencing all the consonant actions on the Empty Chart. Perhaps the thought is, "I haven't felt a trill in a while," or "I wonder what a fricative would feel like back there." Also, remember your non-pulmonics! Finally, remember that phthong varieties are infinite, so if you find yourself gravitating to just a few or to just the ones in your language(s), mix it up!

As you build this new (slightly) narrowed language, the goal is to achieve as much variety as possible within it. We will call this new language **Omnish**, which comes from the Latin word "omnes," meaning "all." As such, Omnish will include *all* of the consonant and phthong sounds that could exist in real, human language. It's a powerful tool we will continue to refine throughout this text.

Reflection

In Module Five, we asked you to consider what outrageous vocal tract sounds might not occur in language. Now, consider what sounds might be found in Outlandish but not in Omnish. For one, the Empty Chart will determine what consonants are part of Omnish. Are there any trends you can identify? Revisit some hypotheses (and the warning) on page 60 to help kick-start this reflection.

Exercise 2A: Omnish—Clinical Version, Solo

Web Resource 14: Printable Empty Consonant Charts

You will need a printed copy of the Empty Chart (both pulmonic and non-pulmonic) for this exercise. Recall the "Clinical Version" of your Outlandish which carried no meaning (you did this in Module Four). That was an opportunity for you to explore variety prior to adding the complex layer of communication. This is also the first step you will take with your Omnish, but with a bit more organization. With chart in hand, go back into a flow of freeform Clinical Omnish. Explore both pulmonic and non-pulmonic consonants, as well as the sounds described in Other Symbols. Remember: your goal is to include *all* of the sounds.

Exercise 2B: Omnish—Clinical Version, Pairs

Find a partner to help encourage even more variety in your clinical version of Omnish. Partner A begins speaking Omnish while Partner B, Empty Chart in hand, listens for at least a minute. After a minute of listening, B begins to make gentle offerings of actions or placements they are curious to hear A perform. Without stopping, A takes the offerings by throwing in a few of the suggested speech actions and continues their flow of connected Omnish speech. Switch roles. Try a second round in which the speaker picks up the pace a bit. Notice if/how the faster speed affects variety.

After that exercise, you may remove your clinical lab coats. Welcome to the Land of Omnia where the native language is, of course, Omnish. Omnia is a complex society where there is meaning in everything. Let's start with an introduction to this society.

Exercise 3A: Omnian Tourism—Immersive Language School

In pairs, one person is the native Omnian teacher, and the other person is the tourist visiting Omnia who is committed to learning the language. All interactions must take place in Omnish, meaning *full immersion*. While moving around the room with their student, the teacher identifies objects one at a time and speaks the Omnish word for each. The student then repeats the word in Omnish, and only when the teacher is satisfied that the student has attained a skillful pronunciation of that word do they move on to the next. Switch roles.

Exercise 3B: Omnian Love—Speed Dating

As a class, form two concentric circles. Half the class is in an inner circle facing out, and half the class is in an outer circle facing in—just like the inner and outer rings of the orbicularis oris! Each inner Omnian is facing an outer Omnian. The person you're facing is your first date! You have one minute per "date." Your task is to listen for sounds your date is using so you may incorporate those sounds into your own Omnish. This listening and adaptation are not only to find more variety, but also to find a compatible love language! After one minute, the inner circle of Omnians shifts to their right for their next date.

Exercise 3C: Omnish Politics—An Election

In order to ensure Omnish elections are fair and impervious to interference from outside sources, all citizens of Omnia are encouraged to run for office. Conveniently, campaigning and voting are done all in one day. Today every Omnian is running for the lowest legislative office in the land. Each candidate must do the following:

- Give an uplifting speech elucidating their legislative platform
- Make sure that one or more of their opponents are clearly admonished
- End the stump speech with a big finish

Then open voting takes place in which each Omnian can vote for themselves and one other person. A winner is announced. The President of Omnia may find themselves with additional responsibilities, so choose your leader wisely!

Exercise 3D: Omnish Culture

Omnish Cooking Show: Demonstrate how to make one of the following Omnish delicacies in great, great detail: canned soup, peanut butter sandwich, or scrambled eggs.

Omni-Tube Video: (similar to YouTube, but much more sophisticated): Unbox a new product or create a "How To" video for a new product.

Omnish Olympics: This is a major classroom event. It's East Omnia vs West Omnia. These Olympic games must include:

- An elaborate opening ceremony
- Several incredibly serious sporting events (options include consonant cluster relay race, phthong jump, ice dancing while reciting Omnish poetry, and a newly invented sport)
- Medal ceremonies underscored by East or West Omnian anthems

- Running commentary from Omnian sportscasters, including slow-motion replays of famous Olympic moments

Omnish Radio: Form groups of four or five. One person is the end of a song on the radio. The next person is a DJ, signing off after playing that song. The next person is a commercial. The next person is the new DJ, getting their show started. The final person is the beginning of a new song. Note: this song will continue until someone turns the radio off.

Omnish with meaning is an essential step toward integrating your speech skills from this course into the acting task as a whole. Note that in the aforementioned exercises, you were doing just that. In your role as Omnian, you wanted and needed certain things, and you went after what you wanted with your speech choices. Did you also notice that variety suffered when meaning was introduced?

We like to say that Omnish is the best "tongue-twister" in the world, because instead of practicing only the sounds that occur in your native tongue(s), Omnish trains you for dexterity in accomplishing all the sounds in human language. With that in mind, it's important to remember that Omnish also includes all the sounds in your native language(s). Allow yourself to return to the familiar from time to time.

The skill of variety in Omnish is key. To practice this, continue to toggle back and forth between Clinical Omnish and Omnish with meaning in class and in your private practice. That way, you'll know you're always increasing your Omnish vocabulary and thereby increasing your speech flexibility and adventurousness!

Let's toggle to the more clinical now.

Exercise 4: Omnish—Clinical Version, Solo Redux

Revisit your solo Clinical Omnish, perhaps while tracking your sounds on an empty consonant chart. Notice your experience with incorporating variety. Has it changed from your initial exploration?

Exercise 5: Omnish Rehearsal

One piece of your homework is to prepare for this final and very important exercise. Return once again to Omnish with meaning, this time using a piece of text you know *very well* (freshly memorized text will prove too difficult for this already challenging exercise). This text could be anything from a monologue to a poem to song lyrics. One at a time, you will perform your monologue in the language in which you learned it (your "acting language," if you will). Then you will perform your monologue in Omnish. But it must be a *line-by-line* direct translation from the original language. No jumping to general, emotional interpretations of the text. You don't make general acting choices based on emotion in your mother tongue—nor should you in Omnish! Additionally, the speech sounds you use in your Omnish translation should be improvised—not predetermined by you in rehearsal. This task is challenging by design. Then perform the monologue a third time, in the original language again. Were you able to bring over any discoveries you made in the Omnish rehearsal when you returned to the original language? Why do you think this way of rehearsing is an effective tool?

We encourage you to test the efficacy of this exercise across the various languages that may be spoken in your classroom. This exercise is useful even if only one person in the class speaks a particular language. If that one person is able to act in that language and follows the steps of the exercise, everyone in the room will likely experience a shift in their acting without having to understand the exact words of the text. Don't believe us? Test it out!

In this exercise, the obstacle of having to translate into Omnish leads the actor to be really clear about what they are saying. Images have to be specific, or the actor will lose their place. But there is an added benefit to being that specific: the effect is that they try harder to be understood. They are able to discover the *need* to be understood in a completely new way.

End of Module Wrap

Further homework for this module is to explore the efficacy of Omnish by applying it to your work outside of these exercises. Conduct an Omnish rehearsal (as described in Exercise 5) of anything you're currently working on: a show you're rehearsing, a graduate school audition monologue, a scene for another class, etc.

Table 7.1 Terms for Your Module Seven Knowledge Celebration

Omnish
Shimmer

MODULE EIGHT
EXPERIENCING THE EMPTY CHART—VOWELS

After much close attention to experiencing consonants, it may be useful to recall the differences between consonants and phthongs. Phthongs are created by *shaping* the flow with the tongue body, lips, and velum and thereby don't "get in the way" of the flow, while consonants *obstruct* the flow. By definition, they do get in the way—even if it's just a little bit, as approximants do! Revisit the diagram of the oral cavity with the empty consonant chart inside of it on page 76 to remind yourself of approximately where consonants occur.

And now—drumroll, please—let's make an addition to our Empty Charts: vowel space! Yes, we said *vowel* . . . Now that you have expanded your experience of vowels beyond the familiar, we can go back to using that familiar term in all its glory.

Notice the quadrilateral embedded within the consonant chart in Figure 8.1. This shape represents the vowel space, which means that the infinite variety of vowels we've been exploring all fit within that relatively small space. Remarkable, isn't it? Let's take a closer look.

Why is it a quadrilateral and not a rectangle like the consonant charts?

The asymmetrical shape of the quadrilateral aligns with the shape of the mouth more than a symmetrical rectangle does. The bottom of the mouth tends to be shorter than the roof of the mouth, meaning that for most

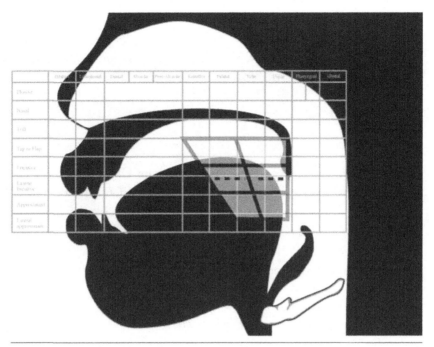

Figure 8.1 The Empty Charts in the Mouth

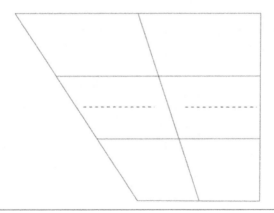

Figure 8.2 The Empty Vowel Quadrilateral

folks, the lower front teeth are behind the upper front teeth. It also has to do with the fact that the cupping action of the tongue is constrained within the space of the mandible, but the arching action of the tongue reaches up out of the jaw and so adds a bit more range of motion.

Special Note

We say "most folks" because this shape is a *representation* of vowel space. It's not "the correct" shape, or even the shape of everyone's vowel space.

Just as with the Empty (pulmonic) Consonant Chart, this quadrilateral represents a person facing left. The left side of the Empty Vowel Chart represents the front of the mouth, and the right side represents the back of the mouth. The top line of the quadrilateral represents the space just below the roof of the mouth, and the bottom line represents the space just above the bottom of the mouth.

What are those other horizontal lines inside the quadrilateral?
And the vertical slanted line going down the middle?

Since this Empty Vowel Chart represents the vowel space, that means that any single point within this quadrilateral is a location inside the mouth where some part of the tongue body could go to shape a vowel. Those lines are like longitude and latitude lines on a tongue map.

What does that mean?

Remember the Equator Tongue from Module Two? This dotted line in Figure 8.2 is our equator. In this vowel space, it represents where the tongue is when it's completely flat. Create that flat shape with your tongue now. Breathe in to feel the cool air over the top surface of the tongue. Adjust as needed to make sure it's as flat as possible, and keep your lips relaxed. Now, simultaneously trace the dotted line you just made on your chart with your finger and add some voiced flow to the Equator Tongue shape in your mouth. Notice the sound. Notice the vowel. Any location on this chart above this dotted line means that some part of the tongue body has to arch to get there. As we get closer to the top line, the tongue arch is higher towards the roof of the mouth—without getting into consonant territory, of course! Any location on this chart below this dotted line means that some part of the tongue body has to cup to get there. As we get closer to the bottom line, the tongue cup is deeper towards the bottom of the mouth.

What about the lips? Don't they also shape vowels?

They do! Let's start with some freeform phthonging that includes the lips, as well as the tongue and velum.

Exercise 1A: Vowel Space Warmup—Freeform

Start by warming up your phthong variety, shaping a flow of phonation in all the ways you can with your tongue, lips, and velum—without, of course, obstructing in any way. Remember that phthongs use the body of the tongue only. Experiment with arching and cupping the tongue body in all the blueberry rolling or mountain moving gestures at your disposal. Also, remember to find your Equator Tongue and tiny micro movements, or shimmers, around it from time to time. While it's interesting to explore the extreme vowel gestures, it's also equally interesting to explore the more subtle gestures. As you explore, remember that your tongue and lips are connected to the rest of your body. Soften the spots in your body that tend to tense when you're focusing intently on new skills. Breathe. Can you encourage ease in your body?

Exercise 1B: Vowel Space—The Four Corners

Let's pay closer attention to the four corners of the vowel space. Refer to the **vowel quadrilateral** and start at the top left corner.

Think about what that location is already telling you in terms of your tongue shape. We're at the very left side of the quadrilateral, meaning we're at the very front of the vowel space in the mouth. It would be most convenient to use the front of the tongue body in the front of the vowel space. We're also at the very top of the quadrilateral, meaning the front of the tongue body will arch high up toward the roof of the mouth—without obstructing any flow. Try that tongue shape: a high arch in the front of the body. Breathe in through that shape. Then send a flow of voice through that shape. Allow yourself the possibility of being surprised by the resulting vowel sound: is it something familiar? For most speakers, it is! We're trained (and/or hardwired) to get a

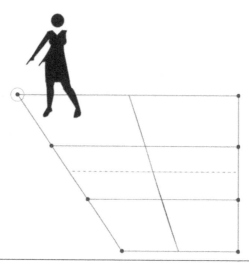

Figure 8.3 Dot Exploring the Front of their Vowel Space

thrill out of recognizing a sound that exists in a language we know. This work has been asking us to turn down the volume on those automatic recognitions so we can focus on the open exploration. But let's take a moment to revel in this one as known territory. You know this sound! You use this sound!

Okay, back to work. Notice what your lips are doing. If they're doing anything, let them relax. Send a flow of voice through that shape again.

Now, let's get the lips in on the shaping again. Keep the front of your tongue body in that same high arch, and round your lips (i.e., protrude your lip corners). Do you recall the muscle required for lip corner protrusion? Breathe in through this shape. Then send a flow of voice through it. Again, let yourself be surprised by the resulting vowel sound.

See if you can maintain that tongue shape and go back and forth between relaxing and rounding your lips. You've got two different vowel sounds with the same tongue shape! For each location on the Empty Vowel Chart, we will ultimately have two possible vowels, depending on the shape of the lips. (Recall that the consonant chart had two possible sounds per location as well.)

Next, let's go to the top right corner of the quadrilateral. We're at the back of the vowel space in the mouth, so we're close to the back of the tongue body. Again, we're at the very top, meaning the tongue body will arch high towards the back of the roof of the mouth where the velum is, without obstructing the flow. Try that tongue shape with lips relaxed. Breathe in through that shape. Then send a flow of voice through it. Now, keep your tongue in that high back arch, and round your lips. Breathe in through that shape. Send a flow of voice through it. Maintain that tongue shape, and then go back and forth between relaxing and rounding your lips.

Now let's go to the bottom right corner.

We're still at the back of the vowel space in the mouth. Since we're at the bottom of the vowel space, the back of the tongue body will have to cup pretty significantly. Think about holding that blueberry at the back of your tongue. Send some voice through that shape with lips relaxed. Then round your lips; breathe in through that new shape. Send some voice through it.

One more corner: the bottom left! We've returned to the front of the vowel space. The front of the tongue body will cup low. Find that tongue shape with relaxed lips. Breathe in through it. Send voice through it. Maintain that tongue shape, and round your lips. Breathe in through that new shape. Send voice through it.

Exercise 1C: Vowel Space Warmup—Mountain and Blueberry Redux

Web Resource 15: Mountains, Blueberries, Hills, and Currants Audio

Recall Moving the Mountain and Rolling the Blueberry from Module Three. To begin this exercise, refer to the sound sample for Moving the Mountain. We've named this "Moving the

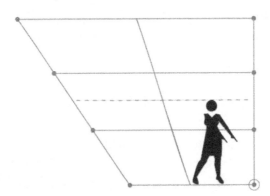

Figure 8.4 Dot Exploring the Back of Their Vowel Space

Mountain," but if it's useful to think of it as moving the crest of your tongue wave, do it! Listen with your ears, yes, but "listen" with your mouth as well! *Important*: do this silently! Don't make the sounds you're hearing. Instead, make the speech gestures you intuit the speaker is making—without adding voice. Repeat several times before attempting those same gestures without the recording, this time adding voice. Repeat several times. Notice that you're arching different parts of your tongue body, and those arches are probably pretty close to the roof of your mouth—near the top line of the Empty Vowel Chart. As a reminder, let the *physical action* of Moving the Mountain be the primary focus of your exploration. Matching sounds to the recording is secondary.

Now, move on to the Rolling the Blueberry sound sample and repeat the same process. Notice now that you're cupping different parts of your tongue body, and those cups are probably pretty close to the bottom of your mouth—near the bottom line of the Empty Vowel Chart.

Next, try **Moving the Hill**. Play the sound sample and listen with your mouth. Make the speech gestures you intuit the speaker making before adding voice to your exploration. You may feel that you're making slightly lower arches (or waves) in your tongue body than you did when you Moved the Mountain.

Finally, let's finish with a slightly lighter-weight fruit to roll. Try **Rolling the Currant**. You know what to do. Play the sample, listen with your mouth, make the gestures, and add voice. You may feel that you're making slightly shallower cups in your tongue body than you did when Rolling the Blueberry.

Look at those solid horizontal lines inside the Empty Vowel Chart. The top one might be pretty close to Moving the Hill, and the bottom one might be pretty close to Rolling the Currant.

Exercise 1D: Vowel Space—The Rest of the Perimeter

Web Resource 16: The Rest of the Perimeter Audio

We just investigated some horizontal lines of the vowel space with special attention to the four corners. Let's investigate the front and back in the same manner. Listen (with ears and mouth) to the Front of the Vowel Space sound sample. Again, **do not** make the sounds on the sample. Instead, explore the *speech gestures* that you intuit will result in the sounds the speaker is moving through. Notice when you feel your tongue passing through the equator, going from arching to cupping or vice versa. Repeat several times before attempting those same gestures without the recording, this time adding voice. Repeat this process several times before moving to the Back of the Vowel Space sound sample.

**Warning

When you model sounds from the sound samples, there is no inherent value in the sounds themselves. The point of these samples is not to demonstrate a "correct" way of making these sounds. The recordings are simply guides to find the *most extreme physical positions* around the perimeter of your vowel space so that later, you will have a diagnostic to determine where any given vowel is in relation to those extreme positions.

Exercise 1E: Vowel Space—Actor's Choice or Walking the Path

Recall the Obstruent Mapping exercise you did as a class in Module Five and the Empty (pulmonic) Chart exploration you did as a class in Module Six. Both exercises were oriented the same way on your floor. The map of the vocal tract and the Empty Chart occupied the same space because they both represented a human vocal tract in a person facing the left. The vowel quadrilateral can *fit within* that same map on your floor. For this exercise you will need the pulmonic consonant actions and locations placards you used in Module Six. Recall how the empty pulmonic consonant chart was oriented on your floor.

Place the placards in the same order of column and row headers, but take up *as much space as possible* in your room, so that the action placards are down one wall and the location placard are across the perpendicular wall. Within that now zoomed-in consonant chart, tape out a vowel quadrilateral with the top left corner corresponding to the palatal approximant cell within the consonant chart and the top right corner corresponding to the velar approximant cell. See Dot demonstrating this in Figure 8.6.

That is approximately where vowel space fits into consonant space inside your mouth. Now you have a zoomed-in vowel space to explore, hopefully large enough to allow several actors to roam inside of it at once.

Review the movements you explored in Exercises 1C and 1D, Mountain and Blueberry Redux and The Rest of the Perimeter. This time, also walk the journey on your floor vowel space as you make the journey in your mouth vowel space. Walk the path of Moving the Mountain, Moving the Hill, Rolling the Currant, and Rolling the Blueberry. Also review the front and back lines of the vowel space. Take your time. Resist the temptation to get to your destination in the room. Focus on finding the subtleties and nuances of the movement along the journey. That's the important part.

In addition to the horizontal, front, and back vowel lines you just reviewed, you could also investigate the not-so-front or the not-so back journeys of the tongue—or even a diagonal journey that moves through the Equator Tongue position. Pick a journey from one location in the vowel space to another, chart the tongue journey with gesture only, then add voice. Then walk the path of your vowel journey within the taped-out vowel space while making the sounds. Pick another journey. And another. It's your vowel space to investigate!

CONSONANTS (PULMONIC)

	Bilabial	Labiodental	Dental	Alveolar	Post-Alveolar	Retroflex	Palatal	Velar	Uvular	Pharyngeal	Glottal
Plosive											
Nasal											
Trill											
Tap or Flap											
Fricative											
Lateral fricative											
Approximant											
Lateral approximant											

Figure 8.6 Dot in their Vowel Space within their Consonant Space

Exercise 2A: Numbering the Extremes

As we continue to "map" the terrain of vowel space, it will be useful to create landmarks for *the most* arched, cupped, front, or back a vowel can be. Later, these landmarks will serve as reference points to help us describe vowels that are not-so-extreme. We will use a system of numbering the extremes called the **Cardinal Vowel System**. Again, there is no inherent value to these positions other than their usefulness as extreme landmarks.

Web Resource 17: Printable Cardinal Vowel Number Placards

For this exercise you will need the printed numbers and Equator card found in your web resources. As a class, place them on your floor vowel chart as shown in Figure 8.7.

Why are some placed on the inside of the perimeter and some on the outside? And why are some numbers printed with circles around them and some with squares?

Recall that for each tongue position, we can have two different vowel sounds. The only difference in shape would be at the lips. The actual IPA chart includes information about lip rounding by placing symbols next to each other in pairs based on the following rule: "Where symbols appear in pairs, the one to the right represents a rounded vowel."

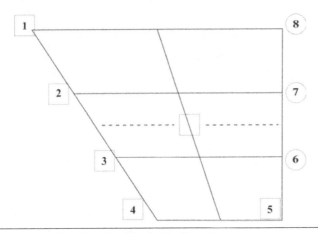

Figure 8.7 The Cardinal Vowel Locations (plus Equator Tongue)

Since many of the vowel symbols appear in pairs, one of those symbols will be outside of the perimeter of the quadrilateral, and one will be inside the perimeter. For this exercise, the numbers with *circles* around them (on the right) represent the *rounded vowels* (with lip corners protruded), and the numbers with *squares* around them (on the left) represent the *unrounded vowels* (with lips relaxed).

Exercise 2B: Experiencing the Numbered Positions

Start with your Equator Tongue—completely flat with lips relaxed. Take this first journey with only breath on the exhalation—no voice yet. Walk a diagonal line from the Equator Tongue card to the #1 card. As you walk that line, let your tongue change shape, but keep your lips relaxed (there's a square around #1!), letting a speed bump and then a hill and then a mountain gradually grow toward the front of your tongue body (we've been to this corner before!).

Since you're traveling on a diagonal line, the speed bump will probably start closer to the center of your tongue; the hill will come a little forward in the body of your tongue; and the mountain will be all the way at the front of the tongue body. Then re-walk that line from #1 back to the equator, again letting your tongue change shape with lips relaxed as you go. On this journey, that mountain (or wave!) in the front of your tongue body will gradually decrease in height and move towards the center of your tongue. Can you feel the shape of your tongue changing slowly? Now take that journey on a flow of full phonation.

Repeat this exercise for the rest of the cards, starting at Equator Tongue and letting the square or the circle around the number tell you what to do with your lips. If you're exploring a rounded number, remember to return to relaxed lips on your journey back to the equator.

Pay attention to all of the vowels you pass through on your voiced journeys. There are infinite possibilities!

End of Module Wrap

It's useful at this point for you to become practiced at the Cardinal Vowels. Do some research on them. Listen to several different speakers model them. You may even be able to find the originator, Daniel Jones, performing them. Notice the discrepancies among speakers! Even though we're mapping extremes, extremes can be relative. In your research you'll find that there are more than eight Cardinal Vowels. In fact, there are 18 of them. Because you can find the first eight and you know the rule for lip rounding, you can discover the tongue and lips positions of 9–18 on your own. Remember, if the number is on the right within its pair, it's rounded, and if it's on the left within its pair, it's unrounded. For this homework assignment, all 18 are fair game.

Create and write down five one-syllable Omnish words using the consonant descriptor recipes to notate them. You will create two versions of each word: the first with one of the Cardinal Vowels and the second with a different Cardinal Vowel. Here's an example of how *one* of your five words will look:

- Word 1, Version 1: unvoiced alveolar stop plosive **Cardinal #1** voiced postalveolar fricative
- Word 1, Version 2: unvoiced alveolar stop plosive **Cardinal #16** voiced postalveolar fricative

Once you have written both versions of each of your five words, practice saying them and be ready to perform them in class if prompted!

Table 8.1 Terms for Your Module Eight Knowledge Celebration

Vowel quadrilateral
Moving the Hill
Rolling the Currant
Cardinal Vowel System

INTERLUDE
EXPERIENCING APPLICATION

We're halfway through our journey of *Experiencing Speech*, so it's a good moment to take stock of what you know how to do and what you know how to perceive. On our journey toward language we started from silence, learned we need to shape or obstruct the flow of breath and voice to make complex communication, and added specific ways to shape and obstruct the flow. You are capable of creating the speech gestures for all the consonant sounds in human language. Amazing. Plus, you have a sophisticated (dare we say "professional"?!?) awareness of your vowel space, which fits inside of your consonant space (look down at the floor of your room if you don't believe us), and you're able to explore the infinite variety of shapes within it which result in the infinite possibilities we call vowels.

You have a vast repertoire, and we're about to get even more precise and sophisticated in our description of speech gestures. Since that sophisticated description will end up taking a lot of language, it will be useful to find a way to compress our descriptions into a denser form. Oh, look! Phonetic symbols!! The symbols aren't more advanced or erudite than a full description of the sound/gesture. They're just a little easier to work with. Throughout this next part of the book, you'll learn a shorthand for *writing sounds*. You may already have your own method of doing this, but what we offer here is much more precise—the kind of precision which will match your ability to *perform sounds*.

But, before we get to introducing symbols, we have an acting challenge for you. The extensive experiential knowledge you've amassed is not just your ability to *make* sounds, but also your ability to *perceive* them, both in your own performance and in others' speech. If you think back to all the exercises you've done in Outlandish and Omnish, you'll know this to be true. Perceiving speech with accuracy, whether you're the one making the sounds or someone else is, is an essential skill for being able to adjust your speech choices, and/or emulate another's speech or accent. Because most films and plays aren't written in Omnish (yet!), it's time to narrow the scope of sounds to a different language (a subset of Omnish, as all languages are). And by the final part of this text, we promise you'll be exploring in the language you're likely to speak in for most of your acting work.

 Web Resource 18: Secret Language Video Sample

Here's your challenge: there is a secret language sample with video in your web resources. It's a secret because we are betting (hoping) you will not know what language it is. If you're a trained linguist and know the language immediately *and with certainty*, please let your instructor know that you're way too smart and they will need to provide you with a different sample. But we're guessing 99% of you will not be familiar with this particular language. Your job is to use all your skills of perception to review this sample, and then to recreate it *with as much information as possible* so that it is a *perfect verbatim performance*. You will listen with your ears, of course, but you will also "listen" with your eyes. What shapes do you see the speaker making? How will you need to adjust the movement of your articulators to recreate *exactly* what they are doing? You will also "listen" with the kinesthetic awareness of your vocal tract. In other words, you'll "listen with your mouth!" This is also a skill you have developed, smart actor.

Why can't we know which language we're recreating?

If you knew, you may come to the task with some assumptions about sounds, and that might interfere with recreating what you're actually hearing, seeing, and feeling. We want to disempower that assumption-maker and encourage you to go with your experience of this language instead.

This assignment will carry you through the entire next part of this book, so create a performance you care about! Also, remember this is a real person speaking a real language, so treat them and their sounds with respect and care. Your performance will be due at the end of the next module. Good luck!

PART THREE
TRANSCRIBING SPEECH

MODULE NINE

EXPERIENCING PHONES, PHONEMES, AND PHONETIC SYMBOLS (OH MY!)

We have finally arrived at symbols! So, what is the purpose of the symbols? Why is a symbol more useful than a description of articulatory gestures?

Reflection

Take a few minutes to brainstorm some possible reasons.

Our reasoning is this: the symbols represent *speech actions*. They are a shared form of shorthand to describe a complex articulatory gesture. You have already learned to identify and perform all the physical actions that these symbols represent. That's the hard part. For example, you know that you can create a stop plosive using both of your lips with either breath or voice. Using the symbol [p] is simply a more concise way of saying "voiceless bilabial stop plosive."

The symbols also fit within a structural framework that allows actors, coaches, linguists, speech-language pathologists, and a whole host of other folk to communicate efficiently about speech sounds. With a wealth of experiential knowledge under your belt, you're now at a place in your speech journey where this type of convenient communication about precise speech sounds is useful. In other words, it's time for the symbols.

Cool, cool, cool. Can we dive into them now?

Almost! Before we begin, it will be useful to lay out a few more terms and descriptors that can help us make sense of what these symbols are.

As we mentioned in the Interlude, the symbols included in this module are **phonetic symbols**. This comes from the Ancient Greek word **phone**, which means "sound." A lot of the terms we'll be using come from that root word. Phonetics is the study of sound in human language, and phonetic symbols are used to describe the individual speech actions that make up human language.

It's useful at this point for us to distinguish among the following terms: phonetic symbols, phones, and **phonemes**. Again, they come from the same root word, but they mean different things.

A phone is a single unit of speech, regardless of its function in language.

A phoneme is a single unit of speech that can be used to distinguish meaning *in a particular language*. The word "ten," for example, is composed of three distinct phones: the initial consonant sound, the vowel sound in the middle of the word, and the consonant sound that ends the word. If you were to swap out the first consonant sound in "ten" for a /p/ sound, the word would change and mean something entirely different in English: from "ten" to "pen." The /t/ sound in "ten" is a *phoneme* in this example, because changing it to another sound will change the meaning of the word. The same is true of the final consonant in this word. If we changed that /n/ sound to an /l/ sound, it would change the meaning of the word in English: from "ten" to "tell." The same is also true of the vowel sound in the middle. If we changed it to the vowel sound in the word FLEECE, it would change the meaning of the word in English yet again: from "ten" to "teen." In this word, changing any of the three phones would change the meaning of the word in English, making all three of the speech units phonemes.

How many phones does the word "lot" have? How many phonemes? If you correctly guessed three of each, well done.

And how is this different from spelling?

Spelling doesn't always follow the same rules that phonetics do. For languages like Shona, Spanish, or Korean, spelling provides some sort of consistent guide to pronunciation. However, since spelling is less precise than phonetics, and languages change their sounds much faster than they change their spelling systems, the spellings of English words like "knight" or "colonel" end up being a very unreliable guide to pronunciation.

So spelling is not necessarily your friend when it comes to describing speech actions. Note that the number of spelled letters does not always correspond to the number of phones in a word. The word "tell" is spelled with four letters, but how many individual speech sounds make up the word? Do you say two /l/ sounds at the end of the word, or one? The word "through" is spelled with seven letters yet only has three phones. Can you figure out what they are? Can you think of any other words in which the spelling features more letters than phones? What about "intention," "knight," or "Mississippi?"

How many distinct phones are in your name? Your instructor's name? To reiterate:

- Phone—any distinct speech sound (and therefore articulatory gesture)
- Phoneme—a distinct speech sound that, if changed, changes the meaning of the word in a particular language
- Phonetic symbol—a symbol that represents a specific speech action

Let's do a quick experiment with our word of the day: "ten."

When you make that /t/ sound, what is happening in your mouth? Describe it to a partner in great detail, as if your partner were an alien linguist. They're new to human speech, but they know a lot about anatomy and they're pretty smart.

Some questions to guide this exploration:

- Are you using the tongue tip, blade, or body?
- Where is your tongue making contact?

    - Back of teeth? Alveolar ridge? Post-Alveolar ridge? Palate?

Now, experiment with how many different ways you can make the first consonant of that word.

If you make the /t/ on the back of your teeth when you say "ten," does that change the meaning of the word in English? What about making the /t/ as far back as your tongue tip can reach? Does any of that change the meaning of the word? Probably not.

Let's try another example.

Web Resource 19: Variations on the /t/ Phoneme in "Lot" Audio

Another word we explored was "lot," and we agreed that there were also three phones in that word—the initial consonant, the vowel in the middle, and the final consonant. What if we didn't use our tongue to make the final /t/ sound? What if we used a glottal stop plosive? Would that change the meaning of the word in English? And does that feel familiar to you at all? Try using some of the different /t/ sounds you found in our last exploration here. Would a retroflex, a dental, or a post-alveolar /t/ at the end of "lot" change the meaning of the word?

It wouldn't change the meaning of the word, but all of those /t/ sounds are wildly different. How can they all be considered a /t/?

Now you're on to something! While variations of a phoneme may not change the *meaning* of a word, we can all agree that the individual variations are different articulatory gestures, yes? When you make a /t/ on the back of your teeth, you can feel and hopefully hear the difference between that gesture and what it feels/sounds like to make a /t/ on your alveolar ridge. These differing physical realizations of the /t/ phoneme are called **allophones**. They are different articulatory gestures, but they do not change the meaning of the word. We could imagine the phoneme /t/ as being a bucket, and all of the articulatory gestures we might use to communicate a /t/ are objects inside of that bucket. Or we might imagine the phoneme /t/ as being a primary color category like "blue." The different articulatory gestures we might use to communicate /t/ are different shades of blue like navy or turquoise, but they all belong to the "blue" category. We recognize all of these versions of /t/ as belonging to the same category: a *phonemic* category.

If all possible allophones of the phoneme /t/ are represented by the same letter in the spelling of the word, how can we communicate to another actor, or to ourselves, that we want to use one particular gesture for /t/ rather than another?

Phonetic symbols allow us to be specific about exactly what's missing in spelling and in our phonemic understanding of speech sounds. If Sade makes their /t/ sound on the back of their teeth, and Soren makes their /t/ sound with the tip of their tongue reaching up to the palate (aka retroflex), and Sophie makes their /t/ sound using a glottal stop plosive, we have a way of describing those sounds we're hearing with separate phonetic symbols.

Exercise 1: Finding Different Phonemes

Pick a word amongst yourselves. Could be a fancy word or an everyday word, but make it a real word. Write it somewhere everyone can see it and take turns saying it out loud. Does everyone say it exactly the same way? Recall that *phonemes* tell us the categories of meaning being used to make the word (the bucket or the primary color category), and as a class you're probably all agreeing on the phonemes that make up the word. We can use *phonetic symbols* to communicate *how* those sounds are being made by each individual (the allophones), because within your class we venture to guess that there is some allophonic variation in how each person is realizing some of the phonemes in the word.

I've noticed you show the symbols in two different ways—sometimes with slashes and sometimes with brackets. Are they interchangeable?

No! But that's a very astute observation. When we use symbols to describe phonemes, we'll put slashes around them: /t/.

When we use symbols to describe allophones, we'll put brackets around them: [t].

More on this when we get the symbols.

Interlude Performance Time!

Perform your language sample from the interlude module with *as much detail as possible*. After each person has performed, discuss some of the techniques you employed to tackle this task.

End of Module Wrap

Your homework for this module is to explore how shifting one *phoneme* at a time can completely change a word's meaning. You explored this last module by changing the Cardinal Vowels in Omnish words. We're going to finish this module with a game we call Chain Linking.

Begin with a random one-syllable word of your choosing. It should be a real word in a language that you speak! Transforming only one phoneme at a time, your goal is to create an unbroken "chain" of word transformations. You will be using the sound description tools you've learned thus far: 3-part consonant descriptors and Cardinal Vowels.

Here's an example of how one "link" might look if we begin with the word "beet"

- Voiced bilabial plosive
- Cardinal #1
- Unvoiced alveolar plosive.

What words can we create by changing the first phoneme? The second phoneme? The third phoneme?

If we change the final phoneme, we can create the word "bead"—

- Voiced bilabial Plosive
- Cardinal #1
- Voiced alveolar plosive.

That's two words—or two links! If we can transform this word into something else, we'll be able to add another link to the chain.

For example, we can change the first phoneme of our new word to create this:

- Voiced Alveolar Nasal
- Cardinal #1
- Voiced alveolar plosive.

Now the word is "knead," or "need!" Those words are homophones, after all, meaning they sound the same when spoken out loud.

Your homework is to create a chain of 5–10 links of words that hold meaning in your language. Can you make more links? Currently the world record is a whopping 27! Can you make links in more languages? Challenge yourself.

Table 9.1 Terms for your Module Nine Knowledge Celebration:

Phone
Phoneme
Phonetic Symbols
Allophone

MODULE TEN
EXPERIENCING THE CONSONANT SYMBOLS

Now that we've got a sense of what phonetic symbols are—symbolic representations designed to describe speech actions—let's look at them!

Figure 10.1 displays our consonant charts. Take a look at the pulmonic consonant chart. Recall that the x-axis represents the location of obstruction—where in the vocal tract the obstruction is taking place. The y-axis represents the action, or manner of articulation (refer back to the river metaphor in Module Five to refresh your understanding if you need to). Location and action represent two parts of our three-part consonant recipe. The third part, voiced or unvoiced flow, is represented on the chart in a fairly simple way:

- When two symbols appear in the same box, the symbol on the left is voiceless and the symbol on the right is voiced. Test it out with [p] and [b].
- When only one symbol appears in a box, that symbol is voiced. Do you have a theory as to why? To test your theory, try making some unvoiced nasals, approximants, or lateral approximants. We'll (gently) interrogate your conclusions when we get to those symbols.

CONSONANTS (PULMONIC)

	Bilabial	Labiodental	Dental	Alveolar	Postalveolar	Retroflex	Palatal	Velar	Uvular	Pharyngeal	Glottal
Plosive	p b			t d		ʈ ɖ	c ɟ	k ɡ	q ɢ		ʔ
Nasal	m	ɱ		n		ɳ	ɲ	ŋ	N		
Trill	ʙ			r					R		
Tap or Flap		ⱱ		ɾ		ɽ					
Fricative	ɸ β	f v	θ ð	s z	ʃ ʒ	ʂ ʐ	ç ʝ	x ɣ	χ ʁ	ħ ʕ	h ɦ
Lateral fricative				ɬ ɮ							
Approximant		ʋ		ɹ		ɻ	j	ɰ			
Lateral approximant				l		ɭ	ʎ	ʟ			

Where symbols appear in pairs, the one to the right represents a voiced consonant. Shaded areas denote articulations judged impossible.

CONSONANTS (NON-PULMONIC)

Clicks		Voiced implosives		Ejectives	
ʘ	Bilabial	ɓ	Bilabial	ʼ	Examples:
ǀ	Dental	ɗ	Dental/alveolar	pʼ	Bilabial
ǃ	(Post)alveolar	ʄ	Palatal	tʼ	Dental/alveolar
ǂ	Palatoalveolar	ɠ	Velar	kʼ	Velar
ǁ	Alveolar lateral	ʛ	Uvular	sʼ	Alveolar fricative

OTHER SYMBOLS

ʍ	Voiceless labial-velar fricative	ɕ ʑ	Alveolo-palatal fricatives
w	Voiced labial-velar approximant	ɺ	Voiced alveolar lateral flap
ɥ	Voiced labial-palatal approximant	ɧ	Simultaneous ʃ and x
ʜ	Voiceless epiglottal fricative		
ʢ	Voiced epiglottal fricative	Affricates and double articulations can be represented by two symbols joined by a tie bar if necessary.	k͡p t͡s
ʡ	Epiglottal plosive		

Figure 10.1 The Consonant Charts

Reflection

Before we go further, just look! Look at all of these symbols!!! What do you first notice when you look at them?

Observations may include:

• Some of them look like letters we use to spell words.

  • Some speakers may even say, "they look like the sounds they describe in spelling!" While many of these symbols may be familiar, not all of them represent the sounds you might be accustomed to.

• More specifically, they look like Roman alphabet letters and a few other symbols. Some symbols come from the Greek alphabet as well.
• Some are capital letters, and some are lowercase.

- Some are the same symbol, just flipped backwards or turned upside down.
- Some symbols have "tags," or descenders—little tails or markings that hang off in one direction or another.
- Some symbols are tall, or they have parts that ascend.
- Some boxes have two symbols, and some have one (you know why).
- Some boxes are blank.
- Some are shaded (and you know why that is!).
- There are a lot of fricatives.
- There are a lot of alveolar symbols.
- There aren't many lateral fricatives.

Do you see any other patterns? Try looking at both the rows and the columns. Are there any similarities between the way the symbols are formed and the column they're in? What do all the retroflex symbols have in common? What do many of the uvular symbols have in common? What about palatal? Velar? What do all of the taps and flaps have in common? What patterns do you notice in the symbols on the non-pulmonic chart?

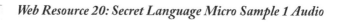

Web Resource 20: Secret Language Micro Sample 1 Audio

Exercise 1A: Matching the Action to the Symbol

Listen to this micro sample of our secret language recording. As you hear each consonant on the recording, make it in your vocal tract. From there, figure out the consonant recipe (voiced bilabial plosive, for example). Then find the corresponding symbol on the chart. Write the symbol for each consonant on the recording as you make the consonant in your vocal tract.

Exercise 1B: Matching the Action to the Symbol—Partner Version

With a partner, decide who will be Partner A and Partner B. A's job is to pick, at random or according to their curiosity, one consonant at a time from the chart. They may choose from any part of the chart: the pulmonic chart, the non-pulmonic chart, or other symbols. A makes the consonant they have chosen. B's job is to repeat the sound that A is making and then find the symbol for it on the chart. Both partners then write the symbol for that consonant. After A has picked five consonants, switch roles.

Exercise 2A: Consonants in Words—Group Version

Let's revisit some of the words we were playing with in the last module, now that we have the consonant symbols at our disposal. Start with "ten." Say the word a few times with the goal of identifying the consonants in it. What is the recipe for the initial consonant? Once you have figured that out, find the IPA symbol that represents that recipe. Then do the same with the final consonant. Write both symbols, leaving a blank space for the vowel for now.

Now, repeat that process with the word "lot." Is everyone in the group making these consonants in the same way? Perhaps take a moment for each person to say it out loud and listen for potential differences. If there are differences, simply notice them for now, and look for a broader phonemic category to decide which symbol to use. We'll come back to those differences later.

What about the word "through?" What are the consonants in that word?

Then, try these words: "knight," "intention," and "Mississippi."

Exercise 2B: Consonants in Omnish Words—Group Version

Take turns coming up with some one-syllable Omnish words. When you offer one to the group, make sure you can repeat it exactly as you said it the first time. As a group, figure out where the consonants are in the word. Then figure out the recipes for those consonants. Then the symbols. Write them down.

Exercise 2C: Consonants in Your First and Last Names

Identify only the consonants in your first and last names, according to how you say them. Write—or **transcribe**—the IPA symbols for them, leaving blank spaces for the vowels. Share your transcriptions with the group.

End of Module Wrap
HOMEWORK PROJECT:

Web Resource 21: Secret Language Micro Sample 2 Audio

Using another micro sample of our secret language recording, listen (many, many times). As you listen, try some different strategies:

- Listen in a quiet space.
- Listen with headphones.
- Listen with your mouth. Talk along with the sample, making the sounds you're hearing. Do this on a flow of breath or on a flow of phonation.
- Listen to a slowed-down version of the sample.

Create an initial **phonetic transcription** of the consonant sounds in your sample. For now, leave the vowel spaces blank with an underscore, so our favorite example word ("ten") would be transcribed as [t__n]. Because you'll be transcribing the exact consonant actions you hear, use *brackets* here.

Table 10.1 Term for Your Module Ten Knowledge Celebration

Phonetic transcription

MODULE ELEVEN
EXPERIENCING THE VOWEL SYMBOLS

Now that you've spent some time identifying consonants in words and finding the IPA symbols that represent them—including your first and last names and two different sections of our secret language sample—let's turn our attention back to the vowels.

You'll see in Figure 11.1 that we've removed the numbered Cardinal Vowels we explored in Module Eight and replaced them with IPA vowel symbols instead. Symbols have replaced all 18 Cardinals, and there are some additional ones as well.

Before we explore the symbols themselves, let's review how to read this chart. The quadrilateral itself represents the space inside the mouth in which vowels can be shaped by the tongue body. The left side of the chart is the front of the mouth, and the right side of the chart is the back of the mouth. The top of the chart is the space just below the roof of the mouth, and the bottom of the chart is the space just above the floor of the mouth. The horizontal dotted line represents our Equator Tongue shape—completely flat. Any location above the horizontal dotted line will require some part of the tongue body to arch. Any location below the horizontal dotted line will require some part of the tongue body to cup.

And none of this tells us anything about the shape of the lips! Recall that some symbols appear in pairs, right next to each other, meaning the

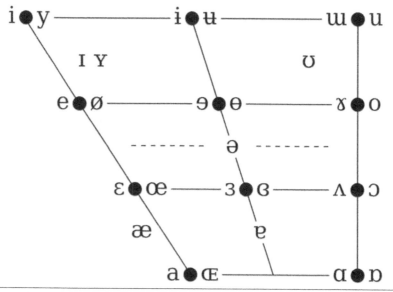

Figure 11.1 The Vowel Chart

tongue shape is the same for both of them. The symbol on the left will have relaxed lips; the symbol on the right will have rounded lips.

Reflection

What do you notice about these symbols? Take some time to discuss.

Here are some things you might notice:

- Many of these symbols look like letters used to spell words in the Roman alphabet. This was true of the consonant symbols, as well.
- One is borrowed from the Greek alphabet.
- One looks like a backwards "c."
- One looks like an upside-down lowercase "e." That one, [ə], is the symbol for our Equator Tongue—the sound that is made by flattening the tongue and relaxing the lips. Try it! The name for that symbol is the **schwa**.

Is the vowel sound in the word "schwa" the sound that the symbol represents?

No! But that would be handy if that were the case. Here's a question: if you were to chart the course from the vowel sound in the word "schwa" to [ə], where would you begin in the vowel space? Front or back of [ə]? Higher or lower?

NOTE: Any of the following exercises for experiencing the vowel symbols can be done in the vocal tract only, or while simultaneously moving through the vowel space taped out on your floor. In your web resources you'll find printable placards for each of the vowel symbols. You will also find location descriptor placards for the vowel space which are defined in this module. Place them according to the chart above whenever you want to explore both ways.

Web Resource 22: Printable Vowel Space Placards

Exercise 1A: Revisiting the Extremes—With Symbols!

Let's revisit the extremes exercise we did in Module Eight now that we have vowel symbols. Start at schwa, and, on a flow of full phonation, slide your way to [i] first, keeping your lips relaxed. Then slide your way back to schwa. Repeat that task for each of the vowel symbols noted here:

[e   ɛ   a   ɑ   ɔ   o   u]

Is there a recipe to describe the vowel symbols—like our consonant recipe?

Yes, there is, and the vowel recipe also has three parts:

- What section of the tongue body is doing the shaping: **front, central**, or **back**
- What the lips are doing to shape the vowel: **rounded** or **unrounded**
- What height the tongue body is: **close** (the adjective meaning "near" because your tongue is *close* to the roof of your mouth, rather than the verb meaning "to shut"), **mid-close, mid-open**, or **open**

[i] is at the top, left-hand corner of the vowel chart. The left side of the chart represents the front of the mouth, indicating the front of the tongue body is being used; therefore, we can classify [i] as a **front vowel**. We know that the lips are **unrounded** for it since it's on the left side of a pair of symbols. It's at the very top of the vowel space, along the line that's labeled **close**, meaning the tongue body is arched very close to the roof of the mouth—but not close enough to be a consonant! Therefore, we can say that [i] is a front, unrounded, close vowel.

Take a look at where [o] sits on the chart. It's on the right-hand side of the vowel space, meaning we're in the back of the mouth and using the back of the tongue body. So, we can classify [o] as a **back vowel**. The lips are **rounded** for [o], as it's on the right side of a pair of symbols. And it's positioned on the horizontal line labeled **close-mid**, meaning the back of the tongue body is arched medium close to the roof of the mouth, not as close as it would be for [u], which is positioned right above [o]. So, [o] is a back, rounded, close-mid vowel.

Can you put together the recipe for [ɑ]? For [ɛ]?

Exercise 1B: Schwa to Partnered Pairs

Each of the peripheral vowels you just slid to in Exercise 1A has a partner—either rounded or unrounded. The tongue shape for these partnered vowels is the same, as we explored in Module Eight. NOTE: the schwa does not have a partner. There is no IPA symbol for a vowel made with a flat tongue and rounded lips, though it is certainly possible to do.

Start at schwa and on a flow of full phonation, slide to [i] again, keeping your lips relaxed. Now, keeping that tall mountain in the front of your tongue body, round your lips. Send a flow of full phonation through that shape, and voila! You have a different vowel: [y]. Notice if it feels/sounds familiar or unfamiliar. Then, relax your lips again, keep your tongue in the same shape, and go back to [i]. Then round your lips again to return to [y]. Go back and forth between those two vowels a couple of times. Then, with lips rounded, slide back from [y] to schwa. Relax your lips when you arrive back at schwa.

Repeat this process for each pair of vowels along the front and back of the vowel quadrilateral, starting with the vowels you slid to in Exercise 1A and then adjusting your lip shape to find the partners. Notice which vowels sound/feel familiar, which might *almost* be familiar, and which feel unfamiliar.

Exercise 2: Completing the Vowel Chart

We have some more vowel symbols to match with their shapes. Close to the upper left-hand corner are the following: [ɪ ʏ]. Notice that they're not quite on the extremes of the vowel space and also not quite on one of the horizontal lines that run through the chart. They're between close and mid-close. In fact, they fall roughly on the diagonal line you slid along to get from schwa to [i y]. So, the arch in the tongue won't be quite as high or as forward as it is for [i y]. Let's try sliding through that diagonal line again, this time stopping when you hit [ɪ ʏ]. Try it with your lips relaxed first, and then with your lips rounded. Notice if either of these vowels sound/feel familiar to you.

Next, let's go to the **central vowels**. Up till now, the only central vowel we've been paying close attention to is schwa—our Equator Tongue. We have two pairs of vowels above schwa, in the center of the vowel space. Let's try sliding up along the slanted vertical line that they sit on. Start with your Equator Tongue. On a flow of full phonation and with your lips relaxed, start to gradually arch the center of your tongue toward the palate until you have a mountain in the middle of your tongue (you may have explored this position as Cardinal 17). Then, again with your lips relaxed and on a flow of full phonation, let that mountain slowly decrease in height, back to Equator Tongue. Now, try that same journey with your lips rounded.

When the middle of your tongue body is arched as high as it can go toward the roof of the mouth (without obstructing the flow), you've found the central, close vowels: [ɨ ʉ]. When the middle of your tongue body is arched at a medium height (a hill, if you will), you've found the central, mid-close vowels: [ɘ ɵ].

Wait, isn't that central, unrounded, mid-close vowel symbol the same as the symbol for schwa?

Not entirely! We have three vowel symbols that start with the base symbol [e]. The base symbol is the front, unrounded, mid-close vowel. Can you find it on the chart? If you *flip* that symbol across a vertical axis—a side-by-side mirror image of it—you get the central, unrounded, mid-close vowel: [ə].

So, those symbols side by side look like this:

[e ə]

If you *rotate* the base symbol 180 degrees, you get the schwa: [ə].

The base symbol and the schwa side by side look like this:

[e ə]

This is one way the International Phonetic Alphabet can get a lot of use out of just one base character. When you have a moment, look back over the consonants, and you'll find similar symbol shenanigans.

Back to the central vowels. We have three vowel symbols below schwa in the center of the vowel space. Slide down along the slanted vertical line they sit on. Start with your Equator Tongue again. On a flow of full phonation and with your lips relaxed, gradually cup the center of your tongue toward the floor of your mouth, as if you're going from holding a currant to a larger blueberry in the center of your tongue. Then, again with your lips relaxed and on a flow of full phonation, let that cup slowly get shallower, back to Equator Tongue. Now, try that same journey with your lips rounded.

When the middle of your tongue body is cupped at a medium depth—holding a currant, perhaps—you've found the central, open-mid vowels: [ɜ ɞ].

But wait—there's only one vowel symbol, not a pair, at the bottom of the center of the vowel space, and it's not all the way at the "open" line. Why?

We don't have a symbol for a central vowel that is completely open, meaning there hasn't been a vowel with that tongue shape observed in a human language yet. And, since that vowel [ɐ] doesn't have a partner, we just have to know that it's unrounded.

Two more solo vowel symbols to go. Let's go to the back of the vowel chart. Close to the upper, right-hand corner of the chart is a solo symbol: [ʊ]. It's between the close and mid-close lines, and it's located roughly on the diagonal between schwa and [ɯ u]. The arch in the tongue won't be quite as high or as back. The majority of experts say it *does* have lip rounding (though there is some debate). Let's slide along that diagonal again, with lips rounded. Start with your tongue flat and let your tongue journey towards [u] as you trace a line from schwa to [u]. Stop when you get to [ʊ] on the chart. Does this vowel sound/feel familiar or unfamiliar to you?

The last vowel symbol to visit is close to the lower, left-hand corner: [æ]. It's at the very left-hand line of the vowel space, and it's between the open-mid and open lines. This vowel is unrounded. We can find it by starting with a very low cup in the front of the tongue body and lips relaxed for [a], and then gradually letting the cup in the front of the tongue body get shallower. Halfway between [a] and [ɛ] will be this final vowel.

Exercise 3A: Vowels in Words

Let's revisit some of the words we analyzed for consonants in Module Ten. Now that you have all the vowel symbols in front of you and have practiced making them, what symbol would you use for the vowel sound in "ten?" Try saying the word a few times, noticing what shape your tongue body and lips are in. Does everyone in the group use the same vowel sound? Are there variations?

What about the vowel sound you use in the word "lot"? Again, are there variations on the vowel in the group?

What about the vowel sound in the word "through"?

The vowel sounds in the word "intention"?

Exercise 3B: Vowels in Omnish Words

Take turns coming up with some one-syllable Omnish words. When you offer one to the group, make sure you can repeat it exactly as you said it the first time! As a group, figure out where the vowels are in the word. Then figure out the recipes for those vowels and the symbols. Write them down. Do you have the symbols you need to accurately describe all of the vowel sounds you're making?

Exercise 3C: Vowels in Your First and Last Names

You've already transcribed the consonants in your first and last names. Now, fill in the vowel symbols—according to how you say them, of course. Again, notice if you have all of the symbols you need to accurately describe the sounds you're making. Be prepared to share your transcriptions with the class.

What about the word "knight"? We haven't figured out the vowel symbol(s) for that yet.

You're right! And that's for a specific reason. When we transcribed the consonants for "knight," we left one blank space in the middle for a vowel sound. Try saying "knight" a few times right now. What do you feel your articulators doing between the initial and final consonants? Try taking away the consonants and just saying the sound in the middle. Is it one vowel shape? Or are your articulators moving through more than one shape? If there is any movement through that sound, it's not just one vowel. It's more than one vowel being blended together to create a whole new phoneme. Two vowel sounds blended together within one syllable are called a **diphthong**.

What if I don't use a diphthong in the word "knight"?

That's perfectly fine. Your accent might not call for one in that word. Do you use a diphthong in any of the following words: place, dome, mouse, or steer? Do you have any diphthongs in your name? If you've found one in any of the above, use the technique of removing the consonants and speaking just the vowel sounds. Track the journey from the first sound to the second. Feel where the first starts and then feel where you end the diphthong. Jot down your theory for which symbols you would use to represent each sound. In the case of "knight," one might transcribe their pronunciation of that word as /naɪt/, beginning the diphthong in the open, unrounded front position and then moving to the near-close, unrounded near-front position. Do those two symbols next to each other tell the whole story of how this diphthong is realized? If you're not yet satisfied by these tools, you're on to something.

In diphthongs, one vowel is typically a little longer than the other. In the case of our word, "knight," one could pronounce it by spending a little more time on the first vowel sound while leaving the second sound quite short. If we wanted a reader of our transcription to pronounce it in that way but gave them the basic transcription above, the reader may not know we meant those two symbols to be pronounced as a diphthong. They might read it as two syllables instead: /na.ɪt/!

What's that period between the two vowel syllables?

That's a diacritic. The etymology of this word tells us that a diacritic serves to *distinguish between* two similar things. Why might that be useful in phonetic transcription?

While you have the tools to identify which symbols to use for each sound, you don't yet have the tools to modify those symbols for a more *detailed* transcription. Ready for more? Next module, you get the keys to the kingdom, courageous knights, including *two* different ways to notate diphthongs!

End of Module Wrap

HOMEWORK PROJECT:

Using the same micro sample assigned for consonant symbol homework in Module Ten, listen again (many, many times) and create a phonetic transcription of the vowel sounds in your sample. Do your best when you discover a diphthong in the sample. Again, you'll get tools for being more specific with them in the next module. You can always go back to your transcription to add *more* detail. Transcription is an art, after all.

Table 11.1 Terms for Your Module Eleven Knowledge Celebration

Schwa	Mid-open
Front vowel	Open
Central vowel	Rounded
Back vowel	Unrounded
Close	Diphthong
Mid-close	

MODULE TWELVE

EXPERIENCING NARROW PHONETIC TRANSCRIPTION

Let's begin this module by discussing your homework from Modules Ten and Eleven. By now, you should have two pieces of your secret language transcription: consonants from Module Ten and vowels from Module Eleven.

In theory, you might be able to hand your transcription to anyone who knows phonetics, and, if they read it aloud, it should sound exactly like the recording, right? *Right?* Okay. Try it.

Exercise 1: Reading Transcriptions Aloud

Find a partner, and take turns reading each other's transcriptions aloud. The task is to *read what your partner has transcribed*, not to perform what you know of the speaker's sounds. This might be challenging because you all have been working on the same sample, but do your best to suppress your theory of the sounds. Be diligent in reading your partner's transcriptions. Guessing ahead about what the word will probably end up being is a skill that we bring to reading. For developing our experience of the sounds as transcribed, however, we need to turn the dial away from word guessing and toward what the symbols are telling us about the speech gestures.

**A Special Note on Reading Aloud

You're new to phonetic transcription. It's a new written form of communication for you, so please take your time when reading aloud. Sound out the symbols according to what you recall of the recipes. If you're wrong, and you make a speech sound that doesn't match the written symbol, *you will live!* We say this in all seriousness because it can feel fatal to get it wrong. But it is absolutely not. Or you may experience memories of reading aloud in class from *the first time* you learned to read. Stick with it. Doing *anything* new comes with a certain amount of discomfort. But getting comfortable with the uncomfortable is a skill of creative geniuses. Onward, geniuses!

Does your partner's transcription sound *exactly* the same as yours? When read, do they sound *exactly* like the recording? Pretty close, we imagine. But are they *identical?* Probably not.

So, after all of this, the symbols don't accurately describe the nuances of each sound?

Well, not yet they don't! What we've explored thus far is known as **broad transcription,** or the transcription of phonemes. This module will explore the tools of **narrow transcription.** Narrow transcription describes the specific actions of each phone beyond just labeling the phonemic category. It describes the specific allophones being used by a speaker.

Think back on the many journeys you've taken through the Vowel Chart laid out on your floor. You've walked from location to location, from symbol to symbol, and as you passed through the space in between, you continued to change the shape of your tongue on a flow of full phonation. You continued to make vowel sounds in those spaces between. As we've noted from the time we began phthonging, it is possible to make an infinite number of vowels.

Additionally, you've already tried some consonant sounds for which we don't have symbols. There is no symbol for an unvoiced dental plosive, for

DIACRITICS   Diacritics may be placed above a symbol with a descender, e.g. ŋ̊

○	Voiceless	n̥ d̥	̈	Breathy voiced	b̤ a̤	̪	Dental t̪ d̪
ˬ	Voiced	s̬ t̬	̰	Creaky voiced	b̰ a̰	̺	Apical t̺ d̺
ʰ	Aspirated	tʰ dʰ	̼	Linguolabial	t̼ d̼	̻	Laminal t̻ d̻
̹	More rounded	ɔ̹	ʷ	Labialized	tʷ dʷ	̃	Nasalized ẽ
̜	Less rounded	ɔ̜	ʲ	Palatalized	tʲ dʲ	ⁿ	Nasal release dⁿ
̟	Advanced	u̟	ˠ	Velarized	tˠ dˠ	ˡ	Lateral release dˡ
̠	Retracted	e̠	ˤ	Pharyngealized	tˤ dˤ	̚	No audible release d̚
̈	Centralized	ë	̴	Velarized or pharyngealized ɫ			
̽	Mid-centralized	e̽	̝	Raised	e̝	(ɹ̝ = voiced alveolar fricative)
̩	Syllabic	n̩	̞	Lowered	e̞	(β̞ = voiced bilabial approximant)
̯	Non-syllabic	e̯	̘	Advanced Tongue Root	e̘	
˞	Rhoticity	ɚ a˞	̙	Retracted Tongue Root	e̙	

Figure 12.1 The Diacritics Chart

instance, and we certainly experimented with using that as an allophone for the /t/ sound in "ten" and "lot." Rather than developing unique symbols for each and every variation, the IPA instead developed a series of modifiers called **diacritics**. Diacritics are added to symbols to indicate a change in how a vowel or a consonant is being realized.

As we've done with the Consonant and Vowel Charts, start by looking at the Diacritics Chart (Figure 12.1) and notice what you notice.

You may notice:

- Some diacritics go directly above the IPA symbol, and some go below.
- Some are superscripts that go high and to the right of the symbol.
- Some of the diacritics are smaller versions of IPA symbols.
- The functions of some might be more intuitive than others, based on the description.

There are quite a few diacritics in the IPA; we're going to walk through some that we, the authors, tend to use more frequently. We encourage you to use this module as a place to *begin* playing with these tools of narrow transcription, and to get curious about how to use the diacritics we don't include in this module.

Let's start with how to modify vowels. For the following exercises, you'll need to return to the taped-out Vowel Chart on your floor and place the symbol placards in their spots again.

Exercise 2: Raised and Lowered

Find the **raised** and **lowered** diacritics on the chart. They look like thumbtacks that go under the IPA symbol. The raised diacritic points up (convenient), and the lowered diacritic points down (also convenient):

Raised: [e̝]
Lowered: [e̞]

For now, we're using [e] as an example; we could use these diacritics on any vowel symbol (well, *almost* any). These diacritics will alter the tongue height of a vowel. The raised diacritic will bring the tongue higher in the mouth. Find [e] on your floor Vowel Chart. Stand on it and make that vowel: the front of your tongue arched a little, lips relaxed. Now, take a step or two up toward the top of the vowel space. Increase the height of your tongue arch as you do so. We've taken journeys like this before! Did you travel into the territory of another vowel—either [ɪ] or [i]? Another way of asking that question is: did you travel from one phoneme to another? Remember that a phoneme is tied to meaning in a particular language. It's a category of sound— like a bucket or a broad color—in which there could be many physical realizations. If you did experience a shift in sound significant enough to change the meaning of a word in your language, come back closer to [e] so that you're in its phonemic territory. You just raised that vowel. We can use the narrow transcription [e̝] to describe the vowel(s) between [e] and [ɪ].

Return to [e] on your chart. Make that vowel sound again. Now, take a step or two toward the bottom of the vowel space—without going into [ɛ] territory. Decrease the height of your tongue arch as you do so.

You just lowered that vowel. We can use the narrow transcription [ẹ] to describe the vowel(s) between [e] and [ɛ].

We said we could use these diacritics on *almost* any vowel symbol. Can you think of some exceptions? If, for instance, we looked at [u], one of the close vowels, meaning the tongue body is arched as high as it can go without obstructing the flow, could we raise that vowel? Probably not without crossing the line into consonant territory, which would necessitate another symbol entirely! Can you come up with an example of a vowel that wouldn't make sense to raise or lower?

Web Resource 23: Raised and Lowered Audio

Now pick another vowel on the chart that you *can* raise or lower.

Exercise 3: Advanced and Retracted

Find the **advanced** and **retracted** diacritics on the chart. They look like plus and minus signs that go under the IPA symbol:

Advanced: [u̟]
Retracted: [e̠]

Again, we're using these vowel symbols just as examples. We could use them on almost any of the vowel symbols to alter them. These diacritics move the arch or the cup in the tongue on a horizontal plane. The advanced diacritic will move the arch/cup forward in the tongue body; the retracted diacritic will move it backward in the tongue body. Find [u] on your floor Vowel Chart. Stand on it and make that vowel: back of tongue arched close to the roof of the mouth, lips rounded. Now take a step or two toward the front of the vowel space and move the mountain in your tongue a little forward as you do so. You just advanced that vowel. Next, find [e] on your floor chart again. Make that vowel. Then take a step or two toward the back of the vowel space and move the hill in the front of your tongue backward as you do so. You just retracted that vowel. Would it make sense to also advance [e]? What do you think?

Web Resource 24: Advanced and Retracted Audio

Pick a cupped vowel to advance and retract. In this case you will be rolling the blueberry or currant.

Exercise 4: Centralized

Find the **centralized** diacritic on the chart. It looks like two dots that go *above* the IPA symbol:

Centralized: [ë]

Can you guess what this diacritic does based on its name? It moves the arch or cup in the tongue body toward the center. Find [e] on your floor Vowel Chart. Stand on it and make that vowel. Now take a step or two toward the center line of the chart and move the hill in your tongue toward center as you do so. You just centralized that vowel.

Isn't that the same as retracting it?

In this case, yes! Since [e] is a front vowel, moving it toward center is also moving it back. We could use [e̠] and [ë] essentially interchangeably in a narrow transcription. You, as the transcriber, might make a choice as to which to use based on what you want to communicate to the readers of your transcription.

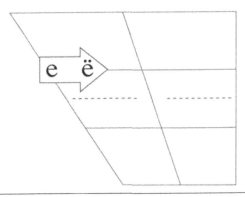

Figure 12.2 Centralization

Web Resource 25: Centralized Audio

Pick another vowel to centralize.

Exercise 5: Mid-Centralized

Find the **mid-centralized** diacritic on the chart. It looks like an "x" that goes above the IPA symbol.

Mid-centralized: [ĕ]

"X" marks the spot! This diacritic moves the arch or cup in the tongue body on a *diagonal* toward schwa. Remember when you walked from schwa to the Cardinal Vowels in Modules Eight and Eleven? You were mid-centralizing those Cardinal Vowels on the journeys from the extremes of the vowel space to schwa. You know the drill. Find [e] on your floor Vowel Chart. Stand on it and make that vowel. Now take a step or two toward schwa and move the hill in your tongue toward center *and* decrease its height. You just mid-centralized that vowel.

Wait, what's the difference between "centralized" and "mid-centralized"?

The centralized diacritic maintains the height of the arch or the depth of the cup and moves that arch or cup toward the center of the tongue body. The mid-centralized diacritic decreases the height of the arch or the depth of the cup as it moves toward the center of the tongue body.

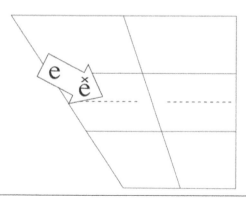

Figure 12.3 Mid-Centralization

Web Resource 26: Mid-Centralized Audio

Exercise 6: Rhoticity

Find the diacritic for **rhoticity** on the chart. It looks like a hook that goes on the right side of the symbol—almost like the hook on the right side of the letter "r."

Rhoticity: [ɚ]

Rhoticity is the linguistic term for r-coloring (or "r-ish-ness") on a vowel. This diacritic alters the tongue shape of a vowel to give it an "r" quality. This diacritic, however, is not explicitly prescriptive as to *how* to alter the tongue shape to acquire that "r" quality. Because of that, we can try a few different strategies.

- Find [ə] on your floor chart and make that vowel—our Equator Tongue. Next, keeping your tongue body flat, bring the side edges of your tongue up to the inside of your upper molars. Remember this from Module Two? You're bracing the side edges of your tongue. Test that modification: does it give your schwa an "r" quality?
- Find schwa again in your mouth, without any bracing. Next, keeping your tongue body flat, curl your tongue tip slightly up toward your alveolar ridge. Be careful of entering consonant territory! Test that modification: does it give your schwa an "r" quality?
- Lastly, find schwa again. Then, keeping your tongue body flat, bunch the side edges of your tongue in toward the midline and gently retract your tongue root. Test that modification: does it give your schwa an "r" quality?

Web Resource 27: Rhoticity Audio

Do any of these rhoticity modifications feel familiar?

Before we move on to diacritics that we can use on consonants, let's come back to diphthongs. We promised in Module

Eleven that we'd go over two different ways to notate diphthongs using diacritics:

- [aɪ̯] We can use the **non-syllabic** diacritic under the second vowel, meaning that vowel is not starting a new syllable and is therefore blended with the previous vowel. Can you find this diacritic on the chart?
- [aĭ] This diacritic is not on the Diacritics Chart. It's in another section called **suprasegmentals**. More on those later. This diacritic means "extra-short." Often, one vowel is shorter than the other in a diphthong. We can place this diacritic above that shorter vowel to communicate that it's blended with the other to make a diphthong.

Let's turn our attention now to diacritics used for consonants.

Exercise 7: Dental

Find the dental diacritic on the chart. It looks like a staple facing down that goes below the IPA symbol:

Web Resource 28: Dentalization Audio

Dental: [t̪]

This diacritic brings the point of obstruent focus to the upper front teeth. We're using [t] here as an example; there are certainly more consonants that could be **dentalized**. Recall our explorations of the different allophones of the phoneme /t/ in Module Nine. Bringing the tongue tip to the front teeth was one of those allophones. You were dentalizing that /t/ sound. Try dentalizing some other consonants from the pulmonic or non-pulmonic charts.

Exercise 8: Velarized or Pharyngealized

Find the diacritic for **velarized** or **pharyngealized** on the chart. It looks like a tilde, or a squiggly line, that goes through the middle of a symbol:

Velarized or Pharyngealized: [ɫ]

This diacritic adds a *second* point of obstruent focus at the velum or at the pharynx. The symbol [l] on its own tells us that the tongue tip makes contact with the alveolar ridge while the side edges of the tongue bunch to allow voiced flow to release on the sides of the mouth. The tongue tip at the alveolar ridge is one point of obstruent focus. Adding this diacritic tells us to also arch the middle of the tongue body up towards the velum, creating a simultaneous second point of obstruent focus, or a co-articulation. Go back and forth between making [l] and [ɫ] in your mouth. Can you feel and hear a difference between the two? Do either or both of them feel familiar?

Exercise 9: Aspirated

Find the **aspirated** diacritic on the chart. It looks like a small "h" that goes to the right of an IPA symbol:

Aspirated: [tʰ]

This diacritic means that there will be a puff of air in the release of a stop plosive. Try this: bring your hand in front of your mouth and make a few unvoiced alveolar stop plosives *without vowels following them*. Do you feel a puff of air hit your hand in the release of each stop plosive? That's aspiration.

Exercise 10: No Audible Release

Find the **no audible release** diacritic on the chart. It looks like a corner that goes to the right of an IPA symbol:

No audible release: [d̚]

This diacritic, which is reserved for stop plosives, elim-inates the "plosive" part of the consonant. In this example, your tongue tip will make the voiced stop at your alveolar ridge without any audible release of pressure. What that means is that the flow has ceased before the obstruction is released. (Say *that* ten times fast!)

Exercise 11: To Release or Not to Release?

Read aloud the words in Table 12.1, experiencing the difference between stopping and exploding each stop plosive (both steps), followed by just stopping them (step one only).

Table 12.1 Omnish Words to Release or Not to Release

BOTH STEPS: [d]	STEP ONE ONLY [d̚]
[ʃɵd]	[ʃɵd̚]
[xɑd]	[xɑd̚]
[ʙud]	[ʙud̚]
[ɲɪd]	[ɲɪd̚]
[t̪ɔd]	[t̪ɔd̚]

How is the no audible release stop different from a glottal stop?

In the transcriptions you just read for Exercise 11, the obstruction was happening at the alveolar ridge. For a glottal stop, [ʔ], the obstruction is occurring only at the glottis, so the location is different. We could also try a glottal stop with no audible release: [ʔ̚]. We could even try a double articulation, making a glottal stop and an alveolar stop at the same time: [t͡ʔ]. If you'd like to test your ears and your articulators, try the Omnish words in Table 12.2 in five ways: first aspirate the unvoiced alveolar plosive at the end of the word, then use your tongue tip to stop but not release, then use only the glottis to stop and release, then use the glottis to stop but not release, then use both your tongue tip and glottis to stop and release.

Exercise 12: Voiceless and Voiced

Find the voiceless and voiced diacritics on the chart. The voiceless diacritic looks like a circle that goes under the IPA symbol. The voiced diacritic looks like a little "v" that also goes under the symbol:

Table 12.2 Omnish Words for More Release Options

ASPIRATED	STOP WITH NO RELEASE	GLOTTAL STOP PLOSIVE	GLOTTAL STOP WITH NO RELEASE	DOUBLE ARTICULATION
[tʊtʰ]	[tʊt̚]	[tʊʔ]	[tʊ͡ʔ]	[tʊt͡ʔ]
[zɐtʰ]	[zɐt̚]	[zɐʔ]	[zɐ͡ʔ]	[zɐt͡ʔ]
[ʌotʰ]	[ʌot̚]	[ʌoʔ]	[ʌo͡ʔ]	[ʌot͡ʔ]

Voiceless: [n̥]
Voiced: [s̬]

The voiceless diacritic removes some of the voicing from a consonant. The voiced diacritic adds some voicing to a consonant. We say "some" voicing because the difference between voiced and voiceless is not binary; it's more of a spectrum with full phonation on one end and noisy breath on the other. In between these two extremes are degrees of **breathy voice**, a mixture of noisy breath and phonation. There is another diacritic on the chart for breathy voice. Find it! Now try moving through the voicing spectrum with the two examples listed earlier. Start with [n] (on a flow of full phonation, as the symbol describes) and gradually mix some breath in with the phonation until you arrive at only breath. Take a new breath in whenever you need one. Then, start with [s] (on a flow of breath, as the symbol describes) and gradually mix some phonation in with the breath until you arrive at full phonation.

Let's move on to another type of diacritic, mentioned earlier in reference to diphthongs.

Notice what you see on this new list (Figure 12.4).

There's that word "suprasegmentals" again. Underneath it is the extra-short diacritic we used as one way to transcribe a diphthong. Underneath it is also the syllable break diacritic we used in Module Eleven to communicate that two vowels next to each other are *not* blended together to make a diphthong (remember the transcription of the word "knight" as two syllables: /na.ɪt/?).

Let's break down the term "suprasegmental." Linguists use the word **segment** as an essentially synonymous term for phone. "Supra" is Latin for "over"

Figure 12.4 Suprasegmentals, Tones, and Word Accents

or "beyond." Therefore, these diacritics describe features that continue over more than one segment and, as such, contribute to the **prosody**, or music-like features of language. These diacritics that describe stress, syllable breaks, tones, linking, and duration contribute a great deal to linguistic meaning.

What about pitch? What about all the tone and word accent markers? Can we use those to denote pitch variation?

Great. At this point, you *should* be curious about all the tools at your disposal. In the IPA, the tone and word accent markers are reserved for languages that use those changes to denote different phonemes. In **tonal languages**, for example, changing the pitch of a particular vowel might change the meaning of the word. The pitch is phonemic in that case, and so we could use these diacritics to describe it. If your acting language is a tonal language, you will use these diacritics regularly! We will play with pitch variety in speech that is more **paralinguistic**—having to do with elements of communication outside of phonemic meaning—in the final modules, when we return to the acting task.

THE INTERNATIONAL PHONETIC ALPHABET (revised to 2005)

CONSONANTS (PULMONIC)   © 2005 IPA

	Bilabial	Labiodental	Dental	Alveolar	Postalveolar	Retroflex	Palatal	Velar	Uvular	Pharyngeal	Glottal
Plosive	p b			t d		ʈ ɖ	c ɟ	k ɡ	q ɢ		ʔ
Nasal	m	ɱ		n		ɳ	ɲ	ŋ	N		
Trill	B			r					R		
Tap or Flap		ⱱ		ɾ		ɽ					
Fricative	ɸ β	f v	θ ð	s z	ʃ ʒ	ʂ ʐ	ç ʝ	x ɣ	χ ʁ	ħ ʕ	h ɦ
Lateral fricative				ɬ ɮ							
Approximant		ʋ		ɹ		ɻ	j	ɰ			
Lateral approximant				l		ɭ	ʎ	L			

Where symbols appear in pairs, the one to the right represents a voiced consonant. Shaded areas denote articulations judged impossible.

CONSONANTS (NON-PULMONIC)

Clicks		Voiced implosives		Ejectives	
ʘ	Bilabial	ɓ	Bilabial	'	Examples:
ǀ	Dental	ɗ	Dental/alveolar	p'	Bilabial
ǃ	(Post)alveolar	ʄ	Palatal	t'	Dental/alveolar
ǂ	Palatoalveolar	ɠ	Velar	k'	Velar
ǁ	Alveolar lateral	ʛ	Uvular	s'	Alveolar fricative

OTHER SYMBOLS

ʍ Voiceless labial-velar fricative
w Voiced labial-velar approximant
ɥ Voiced labial-palatal approximant
ʜ Voiceless epiglottal fricative
ʢ Voiced epiglottal fricative
ʡ Epiglottal plosive

ɕ ʑ Alveolo-palatal fricatives
ɺ Voiced alveolar lateral flap
ɧ Simultaneous ʃ and x

Affricates and double articulations can be represented by two symbols joined by a tie bar if necessary.

k͡p t͡s

VOWELS

Front   Central   Back

Close   i • y   ɨ • ʉ   ɯ • u
              ɪ Y   ʊ
Close-mid   e • ø   ɘ • ɵ   ɤ • o
                        ə
Open-mid   ɛ • œ   ɜ • ɞ   ʌ • ɔ
                  æ   ɐ
Open   a • ɶ   ɑ • ɒ

Where symbols appear in pairs, the one to the right represents a rounded vowel.

SUPRASEGMENTALS

ˈ Primary stress
ˌ Secondary stress   ˌfoʊnəˈtɪʃən
ː Long   eː
ˑ Half-long   eˑ
̆ Extra-short   ĕ
| Minor (foot) group
‖ Major (intonation) group
. Syllable break   ɹi.ækt
‿ Linking (absence of a break)

DIACRITICS Diacritics may be placed above a symbol with a descender, e.g. ŋ̊

̥ Voiceless	n̥ d̥	̤ Breathy voiced	b̤ a̤	̪ Dental	t̪ d̪		
̬ Voiced	s̬ t̬	̰ Creaky voiced	b̰ a̰	̺ Apical	t̺ d̺		
ʰ Aspirated	tʰ dʰ	̼ Linguolabial	t̼ d̼	̻ Laminal	t̻ d̻		
̹ More rounded	ɔ̹	ʷ Labialized	tʷ dʷ	̃ Nasalized	ẽ		
̜ Less rounded	ɔ̜	ʲ Palatalized	tʲ dʲ	ⁿ Nasal release	dⁿ		
̟ Advanced	u̟	ˠ Velarized	tˠ dˠ	ˡ Lateral release	dˡ		
̠ Retracted	e̠	̵ Pharyngealized	tˤ dˤ	̚ No audible release	d̚		
̈ Centralized	ë	̴ Velarized or pharyngealized	ɫ				
̽ Mid-centralized	e̽	̝ Raised	e̝	(ɹ̝ = voiced alveolar fricative)			
̩ Syllabic	n̩	̞ Lowered	e̞	(β̞ = voiced bilabial approximant)			
̯ Non-syllabic	e̯	̘ Advanced Tongue Root	e̘				
˞ Rhoticity	ɚ a˞	̙ Retracted Tongue Root	e̙				

TONES AND WORD ACCENTS

LEVEL		CONTOUR	
e̋ or ˥	Extra high	ě or ˇ	Rising
é ˦	High	ê ˆ	Falling
ē ˧	Mid	e̍	High rising
è ˨	Low	e̎	Low rising
ȅ ˩	Extra low	᷈	Rising-falling
↓	Downstep	↗	Global rise
↑	Upstep	↘	Global fall

Figure 12.5 The Whole IPA Chart (In All Its Glory)

End of Module Wrap

Now that you have a toy box full of new toys, go play with them!

HOMEWORK PROJECT:

Using your diacritics, revise your transcription, getting as specific as you can. For example, now that you have the raised and lowered thumb-tacks, get delightfully picky about the vowels you choose and how you choose to modify them. This will take quite a bit of time and focused attention. You should expect to go through the recording again and again, listening with your ears, but also "listening" with your mouth and your eyes, and with a generous spirit. You'll need to deepen your experience of the actions the speaker is performing in order to make very specific, narrow transcription choices.

Make a goal to add at least one diacritic per word—how specific can you get? Remember that transcription is a communication tool, so think about what you'd want to convey to a reader of your transcription and choose your diacritics accordingly.

Table 12.3 Terms for Your Module Twelve Knowledge Celebration

Broad Transcription	**DIACRITICS**
Narrow transcription	• Raised
Segment	• Lowered
Suprasegmentals	• Advanced
Prosody	• Retracted
Tonal languages	• Centralized
Paralinguistic	• Mid-centralized
	• Rhoticity
	• Non-syllabic
	• Dentalized
	• Velarized
	• Pharyngealized
	• Aspirated
	• No audible release
	• Breathy voice

PART FOUR
SPEECHWORK IS ACTING WORK

MODULE THIRTEEN
EXPERIENCING ORAL POSTURE

Before the big reveal of our Secret Language Sample, let's do a group investigation of your narrow transcriptions. Find a way to look at all the transcriptions from the class, anonymously. We suggest creating a shared, web-based document where everyone can contribute their transcription without revealing their identity. Are they all identical? We guarantee they are not! We'd be shocked if they were! Do they all use the symbols and diacritics as they were designed to be used? Perhaps not. But they are all trying to communicate something very specific: *your experience of the sound sample*. Your experience is complex and nuanced and thoughtful, and you have tools to communicate that experience. Consider that each person's transcription is a way for them to say, "These are some things I'm noticing."

Exercise 1: Narrow Transcription→ Listen, Read, Discuss

As a class, play the sound sample twice for each transcription, and read each transcription twice along with the playback.

Reflection

Notice some things others included in their transcriptions that you might want to adopt. Notice

> where you disagree with your esteemed colleagues. Notice some
> uses of symbols that are confusing to you. Take some time to dis-
> cuss as a group.

I get there's no right or wrong way to speak or to investigate.
I'm there with you. But isn't there a right or wrong, really, when it comes
to phonetic transcription? Be honest.

Oh, you got us. Yes. It is completely possible to be completely and utterly
wrong in phonetic transcription. But we will double down on this idea:
"Getting It Wrong Is Getting It Right."

There are two types of wrong. First, there's the kind of wrong that's
novice wrong. You're new to phonetic transcription, and this kind of
wrong is expected from time to time. For example, if you forgot you were
transcribing and not spelling, we would consider that to be novice wrong.
No shame in being novice wrong. It's non-fatal! Getting it novice wrong
this time means getting it right next time. Adjust and move forward
without judgment.

The other kind of wrong is actually our favorite kind of wrong. That's
interesting wrong. It's interesting to use your phonetic transcription to
make your classmates think deeply about the sounds you're describing.
The class might be split down the middle, each side raising their voices in
passionate argument for or against your daring use of a laminal rather than
a dental diacritic. That's interesting! In this case, it's really not *wrong* at all.
In fact, getting it *right* is not even the goal! You're winning in a different
way. You're making a bold choice and inciting debate. Again, interesting.

What Exactly Did It Take for You to Analyze
the Sound Sample With That Level of Detail?

We think there's a technique or ability you used that isn't quite listening,
or describing, or recognizing. We think it's deeper than that. Most likely,
you *embodied* the sounds you heard. This is such a *fundamental human
ability* that it's easy to overlook. We've asked you before in this book to
"listen with your mouth," and we offered that suggestion with little expla-
nation because we're confident that you have that ability.

The embodiment you practiced is a superpower that humans possess, but it was refined by the various experiences you've had throughout this text that toggled between embodiment and description. Here we are again: back and forth from deep investigation, interrogation, and isolation to audacious and adventurous application. Or analysis that leads to play that leads to analysis that leads to play (that leads to analysis).

In replicating the sounds from our Secret Language Sample, you made some changes to the shape of your vocal tract—or **oral posture.** Oral posture is the physicality that shapes an accent or a language. If you possess the superpower of being fluent in more than one language, you probably shift between oral postures intuitively. Think of oral posture as the home base for an accent. It's not a fixed, held position, like the posture of a statue—but rather, the posture of a runner about to leave the blocks. It's any given speaker's relaxed state of readiness, waiting for the starting gun of an idea to set their articulators into action. We asked you in Module Seven to consider your own home base when speaking Omnish. Consider it again now by speaking the sound sample in your own accent.

Exercise 2: Deconstructing Oral Posture

First, speak the lines of the sound sample, yet again, recreating the speaker's sounds as precisely as possible. You must have it memorized by now! Now, speak the lines of the sample again, this time, as if coming *from your own accent.* What physical changes did you have to make to do so? Below are a few things to consider.

Did you change:

- Jaw height?
- Jaw advancement or retraction?
- Tongue-arching or cupping? If so, how cupped? How arched?
- Tongue root advancement or retraction?
- Tongue spreading or bunching? Bracing?
- Lip corner position? If so, more retracted or protruded?
- Lip pursing?
- Velum height?
- Cheek tension? If so, more tense or less lax? And where? The whole cheek? Just behind the lip corners?

With this exercise you are reactivating your connection to the familiar, and all of your newfound, hard-won awareness is there to observe what you have done unconsciously in the past. We want to say something about this:

AMAZING!!!!

Now go back to performing the sound sample as the speaker does. Take some notes on your theory of the speaker's oral posture.

Cross reference your theory with the rest of the class to come up with an agreed-upon analysis of the secret language speaker's oral posture. There may be dissention since, after all, you're all coming from your own different oral postures to arrive at the speaker's. But some trends will emerge.

Exercise 3: Omnish and Oral Posture

Take one minute now to revisit your Omnish. Let it be a comfortably paced, Clinical Omnish—not for meaning-making but for warming up all the speech actions in human language. Rest. Now consider your own oral posture and how it affects your Omnish.

Is my oral posture the thing that makes my Omnish sound different from my classmates' Omnish?

Possibly! It's not altogether uncommon for one speaker's Omnish to sound altogether different from another's. Let's intensify that difference as an experiment.

Exercise 4: Omnish and Intensified Oral Posture

Exaggerate your oral posture. If you noticed you had some lip corner retraction, double it. If you noticed a tendency for your tongue to be arched in the back and retracted, do more. Shift the posture enough to make a significant difference in the shapes you make, but retain the ability to flow in connected language. Begin another minute of Omnish now.

You are, by default, self-selecting some sounds over others as this new oral posture allows some speech gestures to be made easily, and others not so easily. It's no longer *all* the sounds in human language. It's only *some* of them. It's no longer Omnish (all sounds), but **Somenish** (some of the sounds).

Exercise 5: Somenish Into Acting Language

Go back into the Somenish of your intensified oral posture. Talk about the last meal you ate. After about a minute, transition into your **Acting Language**, the language you're using for most of your acting, bringing some of the gestural vocabulary of the Somenish oral posture into your Acting Language. Continue to describe that meal.

What Do We Mean by Acting Language?

We're using the term "Acting Language" as a term of art. What we mean is the language(s) you'll be using in your acting in the context of this course. This might be your first language, your second, or your third. It may be everyday practice in your classroom to use more than one language, and to switch back and forth. What we're asking for in this exercise is that you pick a language you know well enough for acting.

From intensifying the shape and movement of your oral posture, you've arrived at a new accent!

That was pretty easy to do, going just by shape and feelings. If accents are that easy to change, why did we need to spend all that time learning anatomy? Why learn phonetics?

The short answer is, "If your only tool is a hammer, every problem begins to look like a nail."

The longer answer to that fair question is that each approach to speech reinforces other approaches. When you learned to speak, you likely began with imitation and exploration and then were introduced to phonics and letters to help you categorize and make sense of your language. As one develops oral posture awareness and sensitivity, more sounds and sound categories enter one's awareness. As one explores the action behind each sound and sound category, the oral posture gets more specific and accurate.

For the final time, revisit your class's oral posture analysis for the Secret Language Speaker.

Exercise 6: Secret Language Into Acting Language (With Memorized Text)

Last time, we promise: speak the lines of the sound sample recreating the speaker's sounds as precisely as possible, paying close attention to the oral posture tendencies you agreed upon as a class. After about a minute, transition into your Acting Language, again bringing some of the gestural vocabulary of the Secret Language oral posture into your Acting Language. Try it this time with some memorized text in your Acting Language. Imagine you *are* the Secret Language Speaker. How might this awareness of oral posture influence other acting choices?

You might have guessed it by now, but the reason we were so sure no one was going to know the language of your Secret Language Sample is that **we made it up. This isn't an actual language.** Rather, it is another example of a playful, improvised Somenish built from an oral posture variation (and, as such, is not recognized by any phoneticians or linguists).

Isn't every language a kind of "Somenish"?

Well, yes. In a way, every language, every accent, is a Somenish. It's a subset of all the speech sounds in human language. We're certainly not saying that Somenish has all the features of an actual language. It's truly amazing how complex an improvised performance of Somenish can be, but it would be a mistake to assume that a full human language could be reproduced this easily. Somenish is sophisticated play, not sorcery.

Actual languages are incredibly complex, and they come with a rich set of cultural associations and grammatical sophistication. And, well, they're real.

But why didn't you choose a real language for this exercise?

There are a couple of answers to this important question.

First, we can't anticipate all the languages you might know or recognize, and we didn't want previous knowledge to affect your growing skills in speech gesture and sound analysis.

Second, it's risky to emulate someone else's language or accent. The way we communicate is incredibly personal. When depicting someone's else's language or accent, there is always the danger of being offensive. After all, there is a long history of accents and speech patterns being used to do a lot of harm. We made the choice to use a fictitious language, and even though we told you it was real (sorry, we lied) and asked you to treat the speaker and their sounds with respect, it's *not* real. If you chose at any point during this process to not treat the speaker's sounds with respect, now is the time to take note of that for yourself. This was a rehearsal with no real consequence. You know that next time, when there is a real accent from a real language spoken by a real person belonging to a real community of humans, you will be more thoughtful. You can go much deeper into this subject when you begin to *experience accents*. For now, know that the skills of deep curiosity, analysis, and play you are building by working through this text are essential for creating specific, thoughtful speech and accent choices for your acting.

End of Module Wrap

Homework for this module is a deep dive into self-awareness of your home base. Write a complete description of your oral posture. Be as detailed as possible, as if you were going to teach an alien linguist how to speak through your oral posture.

Table 13.1 Terms for Your Module Thirteen Knowledge Celebration

KTS TERMS OF ART
- Oral posture
- Somenish
- Acting Language

MODULE FOURTEEN
EXPERIENCING LINGUISTIC DETAIL

In working on our Secret Language Sample (which is not actually a language, after all) for the past few modules, we started with pronunciation (the sound sample) in order to arrive at a transcription. Let's try the opposite. We will start with a transcription in order to arrive at a pronunciation.

Exercise 1A: Reading Broad Transcription

The following transcription identifies the segments broadly and communicates to the reader what phonemes are present. With a partner, take turns reading the following broad transcription.

/ænd ðɪs aʊɚ laɪf ɪgˈzɛmpt fɹəm ˈpʌblɪk hɔnt
faɪndz tɜŋgz ɪn tɹiz bʊks ɪn ðə ˈɹɪnɪŋ bɹʊks
ˈsɚmənz ɪn stoʊnz ænd gʊd ɪn ˈɛvɹiθɪŋ/

Reflection
How did that go? Did any of the phonemes surprise you?

Exercise 1B: Reading Broad Transcription—Maximum Effort

With your partner, take turns reading this broad transcription again, this time maximizing the effort and range of motion in your articulators while still targeting the phonemes as transcribed.

Reflection

Were you already doing some of that maximizing in your first reading of the transcription? If so, why do you think that is?

Exercise 1C: Reading Broad Transcription—Minimal Effort

With your partner, take turns reading this broad transcription a third time, still articulating the phonemes as transcribed but now minimizing the effort.

Reflection

How did that go? What were your successes? Your challenges?

Exercise 2: Reading Narrow Transcription

Again with your partner, take turns reading the following transcription of the same piece of text from Shakespeare's *As You Like It*. Help each other be as accurate to this transcription as possible.

[ən ðɪs aɚ laɪf ɪgˈzɛmp̚ fɹəm ˈpʌblɪk̚ hɔnt̚
faɪnz tʌŋz n̩ t͡ʃɹɪz bʊks n̩ ðə ˈɹʌnɪŋ bɹʊks
ˈsɝmnz ɪn stoʊnz ən gʊd ɪn ˈɛvɹɪθɪŋ]

What do you notice about this version of the transcribed text? How is it different from the version in Exercise 1? Take some time to discuss with your partner.

Does the first transcription have more phones in it?

It absolutely does! Another way to say that would be that the first transcription includes more **linguistic detail** than the second one does. It contains a higher number of individual speech sounds, and, within that higher number of phones, it includes more variety than the second transcription does. It also describes vowels in their cardinal positions on the vowel chart, rather than using diacritics to mid-centralize them or to bring them closer together. Because of the higher number of phones and the larger distance between vowels in the first transcription, you may also have felt that your articulators employed a wider range of motion than they did in the second transcription. Perhaps that also felt like more muscular effort.

So, does that mean the first transcription is the right way
to say that quote?

Absolutely not! It's one way to speak that text, and it might end up being the right way to speak it under certain circumstances. But the second transcription might also end up being the right way to speak that text under other circumstances.

The second transcription contains a lower number of individual speech sounds and less variety, which might feel like your articulators are using a smaller range of motion and less muscular effort. It also uses less differentiation between vowels. Can you identify where in the transcription that's happening? Because of the choices made in this transcription, we could say that it includes more **fluency strategies** than the first one does. It employs a set of strategies to promote economy of effort when speaking. But the choices in this transcription are not the only ways to strategize toward economy.

So, really, which one is the right one?

They both are! Really! Let's try some more things with them.

Exercise 3: Fluency Strategies

And this our life, exempt from public haunt,
Finds tongues in trees, books in the running brooks,
Sermons in stones, and good in everything.
                    —from *As You Like It* by William Shakespeare

Put the transcriptions aside for a moment and allow your intuitive sense of fluency to lead as you communicate to another speaker of your Acting Language. Find a partner who understands the Acting Language of your choice. That means it doesn't have to be the language represented earlier in this module. (In that case, you will have to find or make your own translation of the text. We know you can do that.) Take turns speaking the text, looking for fluency and economy of effort. What choices are you making that might not have been reflected in the second transcription of the text? How specific can you be in your description of those choices?

Exercise 4: Imagining Given Circumstance

With your partner, take turns reading each transcription again. This time, when it's your turn to speak, imagine a given circumstance that would necessitate that amount of linguistic detail or that number of fluency strategies. When you're the listener, pay attention to where your imagination takes you. Discuss. Did you both imagine the same thing? Were you in the same "world of the play?" Or did you come up with different ideas?

Exercise 5: Letting Acoustic Circumstance Lead

Leaving the transcriptions entirely now, with your partner, take turns speaking the text four different times with the following acoustic circumstances in mind:

- Performing classical theatre in an outdoor theater that seats 1,100—without a body mic!
- Recording a commercial voiceover in a studio

- Speaking to a taxi driver from the backseat while driving in a noisy city
- Telling a ghost story around a campfire to a small group of friends

When you're the listener, notice your partner's detail and fluency strategies so that you can report back to them when they're done.

Given vs. Acoustic Circumstances

We're exploring two different types of circumstance in this module, and both are the domain of the smart actor. Given circumstances refer to the details of the story, including those of your character in that story. Many of those givens will be illuminated in the text; some you may have to choose based on the information the text gives you. For instance, what kind of environment is your character in? What is your relationship to the person you're talking to? What do you need or want from that person? Acoustic circumstances refer to the performing environment that you, the actor, are in and how that environment will inform your voice and speech choices. How large is the performing space? How well does sound travel? Are you working with a mic? Where is your audience? We must consider all of these circumstances when making choices.

You may have noticed that linguistic detail and fluency strategies don't exist in a binary system. Rather, they create a spectrum with maximum detail on one end of the spectrum and maximum fluency on the other end.

There is plenty of in-between space on that spectrum! And, as we move closer to one end, we gain some things and also lose other things. As we move closer to the detail end, we may gain more information, but we may lose efficiency—and vice versa. Most of the time, the circumstances (given and acoustic) can help us make choices about what to prioritize. The goal we must always keep in mind when making choices related to linguistic detail and fluency is **intelligibility**. As the Principles (perhaps) offer, intelligibility is a moving mark based on your target audience. It is not one truth held by one person or persons (including the authors of this speech text!). Intelligibility is about communication, and communication is both giving and receiving. It is a relationship between speaker and listener. Whatever skills we deploy in our speech must be guided by the changing needs for communication within that relationship.

Here are some questions you can ask yourself as you come to a decision about how to be intelligible in any given context. Can you come up with more?

- What is right for the circumstance of the script?
- What is the performance venue?
- What is the medium or media (live in-person play, live online play, voiceover, TV, film, or social media)?
- Who is our audience? And what will help them understand us?

End of Module Wrap

Homework:

Craft your own given and acoustic circumstances using the text from this module. If you possess the superpower of being able to act in more than one language, you may want to find or make a translation of this text in the language of your choosing. Rehearse it, committing fully to your choice. Be prepared to share your work and your process with the group. Some things to consider during that process are:

- What are the circumstances you've chosen?
- How did those choices affect your degree of detail and fluency?
- Did anything about the circumstances or detail/fluency change for you as you rehearsed?

Table 14.1 Terms for Your Module Fourteen Knowledge Celebration

KTS TERMS OF ART
- Linguistic Detail
- Fluency Strategy
- Intelligibility

Module Fifteen
Experiencing Strategy

Let's get more specific about linguistic detail and fluency strategies. What exactly are the things we can adjust in our own speech to move back and forth along the detail/fluency spectrum? We'll start with your own actor's intuition on what they might be, using the following monologue.

> That's where you're wrong. I do love them. But that's not the important part. I respect them. I have never met a person more loyal to their friends and family, who values honesty, and who genuinely looks for the good in everyone. I admire their positivity and their ability to strive for the best no matter what. I trust them to make decisions based not only on the betterment of their own situation, but that of the big picture as a whole. I revere them for their bravery to take a risk and try something new, to battle a challenge and come out on the other end unscathed. That's the person I care about.
>
> From "Giving Thanks" by Adriano Cabral

Exercise 1: Intuiting Linguistic Detail

With a partner, take turns speaking the monologue just presented with as much linguistic detail as you can—whatever that means to you right now. After you each take a turn speaking and listening, have a conversation about what you observed. What were some of the features contributing to greater linguistic detail?

Exercise 2: Intuiting Fluency Strategies

With your partner, take turns speaking the monologue with as many fluency strategies as you can—whatever that means to you right now. After you each take a turn speaking and listening, have a conversation about what you observed. What were some of the features contributing to greater fluency? Could you go even further and still be intelligible? Let's try it!

Exercise 3: Intuiting Intelligibility

With your partner, take turns speaking the monologue with even more fluency strategies than you did in Exercise 2—whatever that means to you right now. After you each take a turn speaking and listening, have a conversation about what you observed. Did you cross the threshold into no longer being intelligible? What is it to toe that line with your partner as your audience?

Bonus Round!

With your partner, again take turns speaking the monologue. This time, can you find even more linguistic detail than you did in Exercise 1?

Since we, the authors, sadly aren't there to witness your work with your partner, we'll list here some variables that can contribute to linguistic detail and some fluency strategies that we've encountered:

- Number of phones: increasing the number of articulatory gestures increases the linguistic detail. Decreasing the number of articulatory gestures is a fluency strategy. For instance, if you encounter a word that has a consonant cluster in it (i.e., more than one consonant in a row, with no vowels in between), you might not always fully articulate each consonant in that cluster. Here are a few examples in English:

> friendly
> consonant
> twenty

Try saying each of these words with more and then less linguistic detail. The number of phones can also be influenced by the articulation (or lack thereof) of vowels. Try saying the following words with less and then more linguistic detail:

> diary
> camera
> garden

- Amount of muscular effort: bringing more muscular engagement and a larger range of motion to articulators might increase linguistic detail. Bringing more relaxation and a smaller range of motion to articulators might be a fluency strategy.
- Variety of phones: including a wider variety of speech sounds, or making more differentiation among your inventory of vowels and consonants, increases linguistic detail. Including a smaller variety of speech sounds might be a fluency strategy. For example, try saying these two words back-to-back: "writer" and "rider." How similar or different do they sound? Can you adjust your phone variety to go the other way with them—either make them sound more the same or more different? Now, try saying these two words: "pin" and "pen." Then adjust as needed to either increase or decrease your phone variety.
- Prosodic features: including a wider variety of pitch, rate, and volume increases linguistic detail. Including less variety of pitch, rate, and volume is a fluency strategy.
- Oral posture: choosing a posture that allows for a larger number of phones and more variety of phones increases linguistic detail. Choosing a posture that facilitates a smaller number of phones with less variety is a fluency strategy.

Reflection

Can you think of other variables that contribute to linguistic detail and fluency?

Exercise 4: Playing With Sliders

Find a partner again and write each of the following variables on its own piece of paper:

- Number of phones
- Muscular effort
- Variety of phones
- Pitch variety
- Volume variety
- Rate variety
- Jaw height
- Velum height

Let's put these variables into action using a memorized text of your choosing. One of you will be the speaker. One of you will be the Detail/ Fluency DJ. As the DJ, you will operate a "slider" (like on a mixing board) for each of the variables listed, one at a time.

The speaker is in the studio, and the DJ, standing about 10 paces away, is in the booth facing the speaker. The DJ should pre-set all variables to 5 on a scale of 1–10, placing the placards about halfway between booth and studio. If the DJ picks up a variable placard and takes one step toward the speaker, that slider is now at 6. If the DJ takes one step away from the speaker with that placard, then that variable is at a 4.

The DJ will choose one variable at a time and hold up that piece of paper to the speaker so they know what to modify. When you, the DJ, want your partner, the speaker, to increase that variable, walk closer to them, one step at a time, while holding up that piece of paper. When you want your partner to decrease that variable, walk farther away from them, one step at a time. As the speaker, your task, as you're speaking, is to adjust only that one variable according to your partner's instructions. Can you adjust these variables in isolation? After you've each taken turns being the speaker and have played with each of these sliders, have a conversation about what you observed.

Exercise 5: Playing With Vocal Characterization Sliders

Now, with your partner and using a memorized text of your choosing, make some other slider placards—this time pertaining more to oral posture variables. Write each of these variables on its own piece of paper:

- Jaw advancement/retraction
- Lip corner protrusion/retraction
- Lip pursing/relaxation
- Tongue bunching/spreading
- Tongue root advancement/retraction
- Tongue body arching/cupping

After you set each variable at a 5, the DJ will choose one variable at a time. Make an agreement with your partner about the directionality of your slider. For instance, does walking towards the speaker mean to advance the jaw and walking away mean to retract it? As the speaker, again, your task is to adjust only that one variable, according to your partner's instructions. Notice what happens to your inventory of consonant and vowel sounds as you adjust your oral posture. Notice what happens to your vocal quality.

Not only might adjusting oral posture influence the amount of linguistic detail in one's speech, but it might also contribute to vocal characterization, or the idiosyncrasies of the way an individual speaks. Perhaps a person's /s/ sound sounds a particular way because of how their tongue habitually behaves. Perhaps a person's speech has stronger nasal resonance because of a habitually lowered velum. Oral posture choices can be another way of crafting character.

End of Module Wrap

For homework, choose two or three oral posture variables to combine. Practice speaking through that oral posture—and remember that posture is not static! Even though you're choosing a home base for your articulators, they will still move away and then back to that home base as you speak.

With a partner, rehearse the following open scene (by "open," we mean that the scene itself contains little information about given circumstance, and so it gives you and your partner the opportunity to make choices for yourselves). Decide who will be Character A and who will be Character B. Start by reading through the scene together with the oral postures you've crafted. Letting those postures and resulting character voices guide you, come up with a circumstance. Where are you? What is your relationship? What's the literal action of the scene? What's at stake?

A: We can't stay here.
B: Why not?
A: It's not safe.
B: You keep saying that.
A: Because it's true.
B: You're overreacting.
A: Not this time.
B: It seems quiet enough.
A: Don't kid yourself.
B: When do you think it will happen?
A: Could be any moment.
B: Or maybe never.
A: I doubt that.
B: Are you afraid?
A: Even more than yesterday.
B: At least we're together.
A: But for how long?
B: Does anyone know we're here?
A: I'm sure of it.
B: Did you just hear something?

MODULE SIXTEEN
EXPERIENCING YOUR ACTING CHOICES

Congratulations, actors! You have made it to the final module in this journey! We, the authors, think that merits some celebration. Let's celebrate you and all of the practical knowledge you have accrued over the course of *Experiencing Speech.*

You now have an embodied and descriptive understanding of:

- Vocal tract anatomy
- Different types of flow through the vocal tract
- Articulator isolations
- Consonant and vowel recipes
- The physical actions of all consonants and vowels observed in language (and some more that haven't yet!)
- The language that puts all of that together: Omnish
- The International Phonetic Alphabet (IPA): the symbols that represent the physical actions of consonants and vowels observed in language
- Broad transcription of speech using the IPA symbols
- Narrow transcription of speech using the IPA symbols—and diacritics!
- The spectrum of linguistic detail and fluency strategies within speech

- How to make linguistic detail/fluency strategy choices to fit a circumstance and/or character
- How to use oral posture for vocal characterization

Wow, that's a lot of skills! Take some time to celebrate! Give a classmate a high-five! Do a little dance! Do the KTS Tongue Dance! You deserve it.

Now, for one final task.

Choose a monologue you want to work on. Your assignment is to perform it three different ways for the class. What goes into those three different choices is up to you.

You could:

- Craft three different circumstances for the monologue.
- Choose three different linguistic detail/fluency strategy slider levels for the monologue.
- Choose three different oral postures for the monologue.
- Or any combination of the three!

Reflection

After everyone in your class has performed, have a conversation about your experiences as audience members. What did your classmates' choices spark in your imaginations? How did you receive the monologue differently each time? What was the impact on character? Intelligibility?

A final assignment (we mean it this time): Here are the Principles (perhaps) or Precepts (possibly) we laid out at the beginning of this text. Spend some time with them. Read them aloud, both alone and as a class. Do you agree?

1. Everyone has an accent. No one's speech is "neutral" or "general."
2. There is no good or bad way to speak. There is only what is good (or bad) *for* a particular context. Speech itself has no inherent

qualities that could be assessed as good or bad. You may *prefer* one accent or pattern to another, and that's fine. Having preferences is human.

3. All humans have preferences. Whether conscious or not, preferences can become prejudices against or in favor of a group of people if separated from our sense of fairness. At this point they become biases. Perhaps we can't ever fully free ourselves from our biases, but being aware of our biases is essential so as not to inadvertently weaponize them.

4. The only baseline "standard" our role as storytellers requires is being understood (unless obfuscation is the goal). But intelligibility is a moving mark based on your target audience. It is not one truth held by one person or persons (including the authors of this speech text!). Intelligibility is about communication, and communication is both giving and receiving. It is a relationship between speaker and listener. Whatever skills we deploy in our speech must be guided by the changing needs for communication within that relationship.

5. Speech training is an essential and deeply integrated layer of actor training, and as such it is part of a complex and subtle developmental process. As with all parts of actor training, the development of skills is not arrived at mechanically or by rote, but by cultivation and play, and by an incremental deepening of experience.

6. A skills-based approach to speech training invites the actor to explore all skills, not merely those that have been marked as socially preferred. Limiting the opportunity to play with the full range of possible speech sounds is impoverishing to the imagination. This work trains actors in the practice of expanding expressive territory through speech.

7. Even though this text is originally being written in English, the work within begins with an exploration of the fundamentals of human language. It represents a universal approach which can be applied to any spoken language. We hope to see this work

taken up across languages and cultures, translated, and continually reimagined as a panlingual approach.

And thus, our journey comes to an end (for now). Thank you, teachers and students both, for your curiosity, your playfulness, and your work. Now go forth and make speech choices in your acting, mouth-letes!

BIBLIOGRAPHY

Adriano Cabral (2017, January) *"Giving Thanks." Giving Thanks*|New Play Exchange, newplayexchange.org/plays/101720/giving-thanks

Dudley Knight (2000) Peer-reviewed Article *Standards, Voice and Speech Review*, 1:1, 61–78, https://doi.org/10.1080/23268263.2000.10761387

Dudley Knight (2000) Standard Speech: The Ongoing Debate, *The Vocal Vision* by Marion Hampton and Various, Applause, Pages 155–183.

Dudley Knight (2012) *Speaking With Skill* with permission from Methuen Drama, an imprint of Bloomsbury Publishing Plc., Page ix.

William Shakespeare, *As You Like It*. The Complete Works of William Shakespeare, http://shakespeare.mit.edu/index.html.

APPENDIX

CREDITS AND PERMISSIONS

Table A-1

FRONT MATTER			
MOD	FIG. #	PAGE	CREDIT
Prelude	0.1	12	Designer: Philip Thompson
			Model: Arizsia Staton
Prelude	0.2	16	Designer: Philip Thompson
Prelude	0.3	20	Designer: Nicole Christine Page.
			Models: Clockwise from upper-left: Shutterstock model (name unknown), Hailey Byerly, Eliza Simpson, Jasmine Vang, Linda Nicholls-Gidley, Charles Denton, Dawn-Elin Fraser.
			Credit to Krakenimages.com/Shutterstock.com for use of the upper-left most image.

MODULE ONE			
1	1.1	24	Designer: Philip Thompson
			Model: Juchun Jay Lee
1	1.2	25	Designer: Philip Thompson
1	1.3	26	Designer: Philip Thompson
			Model: Katie S.
1	1.4	28	Designer: Philip Thompson
1	1.5	30	Designer: Philip Thompson

(Continued)

(Continued)

FRONT MATTER

MOD	FIG. #	PAGE	CREDIT
1	1.6	31	Designer: Philip Thompson
			Model: Arizsia Staton
1	1.7	34	Designer: Philip Thompson
			Model: Arizsia Staton
1	1.8	35	Designer: Philip Thompson
1	1.9	35	Designer: Philip Thompson
			Model: Arizsia Staton
1	1.10	37	Designers: Philip Thompson and Jeffrey Parker

MODULE TWO

2	2.1	40	Designer: Jeffrey Parker
			Models: From top left, clockwise: Cassie Parker, Gustavo Marquez, Ayden Armstrong, Aynsley Upton, Vin Ernst, Miranda Ireland, Steffen Beal
2	2.2	42	Designer: Philip Thompson
2	2.3	42	Designer: Philip Thompson and Jeffrey Parker
2	2.4	45	Designer: Philip Thompson
2	2.5	49	Designers: Philip Thompson and Jeffrey Parker
2	2.6	53	Designers: Philip Thompson and Jeffrey Parker
2	2.7	55	Photo Credits: Andrea Caban, Julie Foh, and Jeffrey Parker
			Models clockwise from Left: Sophie Caban, Charlie Brown, and Cassie Parker
2	2.8	57	Designer: Philip Thompson
			Model: Arizsia Staton
2	2.9	57	Designer: Philip Thompson
			Model: Arizsia Staton

MODULE THREE

3	3.1	59	Designer: Philip Thompson
3	3.2	61	Designer: Philip Thompson

MODULE FOUR

4	4.1	76	Designers: Philip Thompson and Jeffrey Parker
4	4.2	80	Designer: Philip Thompson
			Model: Arizsia Staton

MODULE FIVE

5	5.1	82	Designer: Philip Thompson
5	5.2	83	Designer: Philip Thompson
			Model: Arizsia Staton
5	5.3	84	Designers: Philip Thompson and Jeffrey Parker
5	5.4	84	Designer: Philip Thompson
			Model: Arizsia Staton
5	5.5	91	Designer: Philip Thompson
			Model: Arizsia Staton
5	5.6	91	Designer: Philip Thompson
			Model: Arizsia Staton
5	5.7	93	Designer: Philip Thompson
			Model: Arizsia Staton

MODULE SIX

6	6.1	94	Reference: IPA Permissions (Creative Commons)
			Edited by Nicole Christine Page and Jeffrey Parker
6	6.2	95	Designer: Philip Thompson
			Model: Arizsia Staton
6	6.3	95	Reference: IPA Permissions (Creative Commons)
			Edited by Nicole Christine Page and Jeffrey Parker
6	6.4	96	Reference: IPA Permissions (Creative Commons)
			Edited by Philip Thompson
6	6.5	97	Reference: IPA Permissions (Creative Commons)
			Edited by Nicole Christine Page and Jeffrey Parker
6	6.6	99	Reference: IPA Permissions (Creative Commons)
			Designers: Philip Thompson and Nicole Christine Page
6	6.7	99	Designer: Philip Thompson
			Model: Arizsia Staton
6	6.8	99	Reference: IPA Permissions (Creative Commons)
			Designers: Philip Thompson, Jeffrey Parker, and Nicole Christine Page
6	6.9	100	Designer: Philip Thompson
6	6.10	100	Reference: IPA Permissions (Creative Commons)
			Edited by Nicole Christine Page and Jeffrey Parker

(*Continued*)

(Continued)

FRONT MATTER			
MOD	**FIG. #**	**PAGE**	**CREDIT**

MODULE SEVEN			
7	7.1	104	Designer: Philip Thompson
7	7.2	104	Designer: Philip Thompson Model: Arizsia Staton

MODULE EIGHT			
8	8.1	110	Reference: IPA Permissions (Creative Commons) Designers: Philip Thompson, Nicole Christine Page, and Jeffrey Parker
8	8.2	110	Reference: IPA Permissions (Creative Commons) Edited by Nicole Christine Page and Jeffrey Parker
8	8.3	113	Reference: IPA Permissions (Creative Commons) Designers: Philip Thompson, Jeffrey Parker, and Nicole Christine Page
8	8.4	114	Reference: IPA Permissions (Creative Commons) Designers: Philip Thompson, Jeffrey Parker, and Nicole Christine Page
8	8.5	115	Designer: Philip Thompson Model: Arizsia Staton
8	8.6	116	Designer: Philip Thompson Model: Arizsia Staton
8	8.7	118	Reference: IPA Permissions (Creative Commons) Designers: Philip Thompson, Jeffrey Parker, and Nicole Christine Page
8	8.8	119	Designer: Philip Thompson Model: Arizsia Staton
8	8.9	119	Reference: IPA Permissions (Creative Commons) Edited by Nicole Christine Page and Jeffrey Parker

INTERLUDE			
INT	INT.1	123	Designer: Philip Thompson Model: Arizsia Staton

MODULE NINE

9	9.1	126	Designer: Philip Thompson
9	9.2	130	Designer: Philip Thompson
			Model: Arizsia Staton

MODULE TEN

10	10.1	135	Reference: IPA Permissions (Creative Commons)
			Edited by Nicole Christine Page and Jeffrey Parker
10	10.2	135	Designer: Philip Thompson
10	10.3	137	Designer: Philip Thompson
			Model: Arizsia Staton
10	10.4	139	Designer: Philip Thompson
			Model: Arizsia Staton

MODULE ELEVEN

11	11.1	140	Reference: IPA Permissions (Creative Commons)
			Edited by Jeffrey Parker and Nicole Christine Page
11	11.2	141	Designer: Philip Thompson
11	11.3	142	Designer: Philip Thompson
			Model: Arizsia Staton

MODULE TWELVE

12	12.1	152	Reference: IPA Permissions (Creative Commons)
			Edited by Jeffrey Parker and Nicole Christine Page
12	12.2	155	Designer: Philip Thompson
			Model: Arizsia Staton
12	12.3	156	Designer: Philip Thompson
			Model: Arizsia Staton
12	12.4	156	Reference: IPA Permissions (Creative Commons)
			Designer: Nicole Christine Page
12	12.5	157	Designer: Philip Thompson
			Model: Arizsia Staton
12	12.6	157	Reference: IPA Permissions (Creative Commons)
			Edited by Nicole Christine Page
12	12.7	158	Designer: Philip Thompson
			Model: Arizsia Staton

(*Continued*)

(Continued)

FRONT MATTER

MOD	FIG. #	PAGE	CREDIT
12	12.8	159	Designer: Philip Thompson
			Model: Arizsia Staton
12	12.9	160	Designer: Philip Thompson
			Model: Arizsia Staton
12	12.10	160	Designer: Philip Thompson
			Model: Arizsia Staton
12	12.11	161	Designer: Philip Thompson
			Model: Arizsia Staton
12	12.12	161	Designer: Philip Thompson
			Model: Arizsia Staton
12	12.13	163	Reference: IPA Permissions (Creative Commons)
			Edited by Jeffrey Parker and Nicole Christine Page
12	12.14	165	Reference: IPA Permissions (Creative Commons)
			Edited by Jeffrey Parker and Nicole Christine Page

MODULE THIRTEEN

| 13 | 13.1 | 167 | Designer: Philip Thompson |

MODULE FOURTEEN

14	14.1	176	Designer: Philip Thompson
14	14.2	177	Designer: Philip Thompson
14	14.3	177	Designer: Philip Thompson

MODULE FIFTEEN

| 15 | 15.1 | 186 | Designer: Philip Thompson |

MODULE SIXTEEN

| 16 | 16.1 | 191 | Designer: Philip Thompson |

- All models, photographers, contributors, and designers have granted full permission for use of their image and/or text contributions. Cover Art designed by Phil Thompson. Model: Arizsia Staton.
- Credit for use of a model in PRE-03 (Page 20) appears courtesy of Krakenimages.com/Shutterstock.com.

- All phonetic charts appear courtesy of the International Phonetic Association.

  - To wit: IPA Chart, www.internationalphoneticassociation. org/content/ipa-chart, available under a Creative Commons Attribution-Sharealike 3.0 Unported License. Copyright © 2015 International Phonetic Association.

- The excerpt from Dudley Knight's 2012 text *Speaking With Skill* is reprinted with permission from Methuen Drama, an imprint of Bloomsbury Publishing Plc.
- Special thanks again to Dudley and Phil.

INDEX

Note: Page numbers in *italics* indicate a figure and page numbers in **bold** indicate a table on the corresponding page.

pedagogy xvii; skills, knowledge, and values xi; Terms of Art 22–23, 35, 48, 55, 69, 149, 155; tongue dance 67, 68, 74, 163; train actors xv

knowledge: celebration 15–16, 17, 23; descriptive 36; embodied 36

labiodental 66

language(s): adopting new 81–82; experiencing 79–87; immersive language school 83; obstruents in 59–68; Omnish 82–86; of Outlandish 59; overview 59–60; path toward 38–39; recreating 101–102; secret 101–102, 114–116; tonal 138; *see also* acting language; obstruent ingredients; Somenish

larynx 10; building model of 11–12; muscles of 12; obstruent, making 50–51; understanding function 14–15

lateral pterygoids 23

laterals 64, 69

learning: acting task of xxi; anatomy 147–148; knowledge celebration 15–16; Omnish 83; process 43; states of 36; symbols 73

lifting/lowering, velum 33–34

linguistic detail: acoustic circumstances 153–155; broad transcription, reading 150–151; fluency strategies 152, 153; imagining given circumstance 153; intuiting 156–157; narrow transcription, reading 151–152

lips 6, 7; corner protrusion 25–26, 92; corners retraction 27; curling 26; fluttering of 20; full lip rounding 26; isolating 25–27; orbicularis oris 25–26; phongthing, move/hold/move 44; relaxing and rounding 92–93; risorius 27; rounded/unrounded 119, 120; trumpeting 25–26; zygomaticus 26

"lot" audio, /t/ phoneme in 108–109

lowered diacritics 129–130

mandible 23

mapping, obstruent 67–68, 74

maraphthong 41, 81

markers, word accent 138

massage 81

masseter muscle 21–22, 81

Master Teachers of Fitzmaurice Voicework® xi

master yawn 33, 81

medial pterygoid 22

mid-centralized diacritics *132*, 132–133

mid-close vowels 119, 120, 121–122

mid-open vowels 119

mirrored gurning 20–21

modifier 5, 6

monologue: actor's intuition 156; in Omnish 86; speaking 157

monophthong 41–42, 46

motion 44–46

mouth: empty pulmonic chart in *76*; empty vowel chart *89*, 90

movements: articulators 44; expert gurning 38–39; phthonging 43–44; tongue arching 44–46

Moving the Hill 94

Moving the Mountain 44–46, 93–94

muscles: cheek 25; function 18–34; of larynx 12; lateral pterygoids 23; masseter 21–22, 81; medial pterygoid 22; orbicularis oris 25–26; temporalis 22

narrow transcription: defined 127; IPA chart *139*; oral posture 143–144; phonetic 126–139; reading 151–152; reading aloud 126–129; *see also* diacritics

nasal obstruent 61

no audible release diacritic 135–136

no audible release stop 136

noisy breath 9, 137

non-pulmonic(s): consonants 70–71; empty charts 70–71, *72*, 72–75; obstruents 65, 66–67; printable, placards 72

Made in the USA
Monee, IL
27 September 2022

14753056R00116